Literacy Objectives

2

PEARSON

Longman

Moira Brown
Melinda Derry
Harry Webb

Melinda Derry (Series Editor)
David McLaughlin (Series Consultant)

Pearson Education
Edinburgh Gate
Harlow
Essex
CM20 2JE

England and Associated Companies throughout the World

ISBN 0 582 52989 1

First published 2002
Fourth impression 2004

Printed in China
SWTC/04

The publisher's policy is to use paper manufactured from sustainable forests.

Cover: Getty Images/Laurence Dutton

Sources and acknowledgements

Texts

We are grateful to the following for permission to reproduce copyright material:

Express Newspapers plc for extracts from "Would all our lives be better without television?" by John Triggs and Laura Kibby published in the *Daily Express* 30th August 2001, and "Inside television: teen horror 'Monster Mash'" by Dominic Utton published in the *Daily Express* 14th February 2002; Faber and Faber Limited for an extract from *The Iron Woman* by Ted Hughes; Guardian Newspapers Limited for extracts from "A job for consumers: try to buy nothing" by Laura Barton published in *The Guardian* 20th November 2001 and "Children seen and clearly heard as parents consult on lifestyle choices" by Simon Bowers published in *The Guardian* 31st July 2000; HarperCollins Publishers for an extract from *Angela's Ashes* by Frank McCourt © Frank McCourt; Independent Newspapers (UK) Limited for an extract from "All over the shop" by Jessica Moore published in *School Leaver* Vol.31 Issue 4; Ashley Norris for an extract from "Teenage kicks" published in *The Guardian*

13th December 2001; NSPCC for a storyboard based on *Real Children Don't Bounce Back,* the NSPCC's 2002 public education campaign on child protection; Penguin Books Limited for an extract from *You Don't Know Me* by David Klass; Peters Fraser & Dunlop Limited for the poem "She's leaving home" from *Blackbird Singing* by Paul McCartney published by Faber and Faber Limited; Recruiting Group for an extract adapted from their "Army Officer, Be the Best" advertisement; Times Newspapers Limited for an extract from "Sounding off: little credit for on-line shops" by David Hewson published in the *Sunday Times Culture Magazine* 10th February 2002; and Wastewatch for the extract "How to make a worm composter" from www.wastewatch.org.uk.

In some instances we have been unable to trace the owners of copyright material and we would appreciate any information that would enable us to do so.

Photographs

Lawrence Manning/CORBIS: p.28 (left); Ecoscene/Robert Weight: p.81; Eye Ubiquitous/Paul Seheult: p.6 (top left), 6 (bottom left), 8, 9, 12; Getty Images/Ryan McVay: pp.24, 26, 28, 30, 31, 32, Getty Images/Paul Viant: pp.93, 94 (left), 96, 98, 100, 102, Getty Images/Larry Bray: p.95 (top), Getty Images/Greg Ceo: pp.150, 152 (left), 154, 155, 156, 157, 158, Getty Images/Laurence Dutton: pp.104, 106, 108, 110, 112; Ronald Grant/Universal Pictures: pp.33, 34, 36, 38, 40 (left), 42, Ronald Grant/20th Century Fox: pp.141, 142, 144, 146, 148; NSPCC: p.17; Sally Greenhill: p.6 (right); Christopher Cormack/Impact: p.45; The Kobal Collection/20th Century Fox Television/Andrew Macpherson: pp.113, 114, 116, 118, 120 (left); Recruiting Group: p.74 (top right), 74 (centre left), 74 (bottom centre); Jessica Gregson/The Military Picture Library: pp.73, 74 (left), 76, 78, 80, 82; Moviestore Collection: p.40, (right); John Sturrock/Network: p.95 (bottom); Robert Brook/Photofusion: pp.53, 54, 56, 58, 59, 60, John Phillips/Photofusion: p.94 (right); Popperfoto/Reuters: p.29 (right); Pictor International: pp.84, 85; Hartmut Schwarzbach/Still Pictures: pp.44, 46, 47, 48, 50, 52; 'Des Jenson/Sunday Times DOORS': p.123.

All other photographs © Hemera Technology Inc.

Picture Research by Sandie Huskinson-Rolfe of PHOTOSEEKERS.

Illustrations

Adrian Chesterman (The Art Collection) p.62; Julie Scott (Artist Partners) p.45; Paul Cemmick (The Organisation) p.119 and p.129; Sam Hadley (Artist Partners) p.83; Marc Arundale p.122; Mark Edwards (Artist Partners) p.15; Dan Crisp (The Art Collection) p.132; Dave Williams (Just for Laffs) p.54 and p.55.

Contents

Where it's at
Unit 1: Plan, draft and present

In this unit, you will be thinking about different ways of developing your writing through **planning**, **drafting** and **proof-reading** to achieve a polished and effectively-presented final piece of writing. You will be using your writing to organise and develop ideas, re-reading and revising it to create the effects you want to meet the needs of different audiences.

This process of planning, reflection, and revision will help you order your thoughts and produce organised writing, specifically tailored to the demands of the task. In this unit, you are going to produce a leaflet which will present your local area to visitors and tourists, providing them with relevant and interesting information. The leaflet will be aimed at younger children and teenage visitors.

P Plan

Identifying your audience

One of the first things to consider is the **audience** for your writing. If you are aiming to attract young children and teenagers to visit the area you will want your leaflet to appeal to their interests. This means that your research and planning will have to focus on the aspects of your local area that will attract younger children and teenagers.

One way of starting your planning is to construct a spider diagram, which you can develop and expand to broaden the range of ideas which you identify. One idea, or area, often leads to other, more specific ones.

1 Look at the spider diagram below. One leg of the diagram has been started off. The idea of sport has led to the different types of sport available in the local area, which in turn has led to where the sports take place. Using this as a guide, build your own spider diagram showing the features of your own local area that would appeal to young children and teenagers.

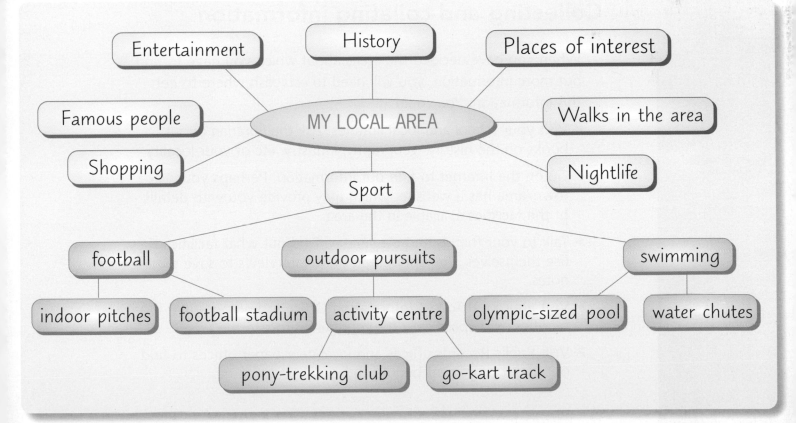

2 When you have completed your spider diagram, decide which features of your local area would appeal most to young children and which would appeal most to teenagers. Choose five features for each audience and list them in two columns as shown.

Example

Young children	Teenagers
adventure playground	cinema

3 The most interesting features of your local area will be the ones that you include information about in your leaflet. You will be able to write about some features from your own experience, but you will need to research others further. Copy out and complete the table below by writing down what you already know about each feature and what you would like to find out.

Feature of local area	What I know	What I would like to know

Collecting and collating information

When you have decided the areas about which you have to find out more information, you will need to establish where to get this information. You could:

▶ Visit your school and local libraries. Ask the librarian about books on the history, geography, industry, etc of your locality.

▶ Go on the Internet to find out information. Perhaps your town/area has a website, which may provide you with details of the facilities available in the area.

▶ Talk to your friends and classmates. Find out what facilities they use themselves. You could tape these interviews to save writing notes.

▶ Visit your local Tourist Information Office to find out what facilities exist specifically for younger visitors to the area.

▶ Visit Public Records offices and local newspaper offices to find out about prominent people and events in the area.

Whichever method of collecting information you employ (or perhaps all of them), you will need to decide how much of what you read or hear will be useful to you in producing your leaflet.

Example

If you were including information about the football ground Old Trafford you would want to include information about how to get there and facts about the team that plays there. Teenage tourists however would not be as interested in the price of season tickets and the cost of parking.

Remember that you don't have to read everything – you are only looking for information that is suitable for your leaflet. If you are using a book, go to the index or contents page to see if the information you need is included. If you are using the Internet, you should make sure that your search finds the right information and you don't waste time reading through useless information.

1 a) Type the phrase 'tourism' and the name of your local area into your Internet search engine. Count how many search results you get.

   b) Now type in the name of a specific place in your local area and count the number of search results you get.

Refining your searches is a good way of saving time when researching. Use words and phrases that will give you more specific information on your chosen feature.

2 Carry out your research using a variety of the above techniques. Whilst you are researching, keep on reminding yourself of the things you want to find out. You should also look for pictures that you could include in your leaflet.

D Draft

Writing for the correct audience

When you have gathered together the information you need, you will move on to drafting the various parts of your leaflet. First of all you need to select from the notes you have made which pieces of information to include in your leaflet. You might want to include descriptions of five or six features of your local area. In addition, you could include:

- quotations from people who have visited the area in the past, saying what they had enjoyed
- a timeline of significant events in the area
- maps or diagrams showing interesting walks in the area.

1 Look back at the notes you have made and choose the features that you will include in your leaflet. Highlight any phrases or quotations that you want to include.

When you have selected the information, your first draft will focus on putting this into your own words. The way that you write up this information for inclusion in your leaflet will need to be:

- accessible – easy for the reader to understand and follow

- interesting and appealing – giving your audience a reason to read the leaflet

- convincing – providing evidence for the things that you say.

2 Look at the following writing techniques that you could use in your leaflet to appeal to an audience of teenagers and young children:

- direct address to the reader, such as 'You must see …'

- informal language using a chatty and friendly tone, such as 'It's a cool place to chill out …'

a) Which type of audiences would these techniques not appeal to?
b) Write a paragraph describing one of the features of your chosen area using these techniques.

Look at the following paragraph describing the Midlands Railway Park for a teenage audience.

Example

More than 2½ miles of breathtaking twisting tracks, thrilling bends and giddy inclines make up the unforgettable experience that is the Midlands Railway Park. Four perfect replica trains whisk you around the stunning scenery of the park's lush landscaped grounds. Don't blink or you'll miss something! After the excitement of your journey you can chill out with a cool, refreshing drink and a juicy burger at the Platform One Burger Bar.

The writer has included the following techniques to add interest and excitement to the description:

- varied **adjectives**, such as 'breathtaking', 'thrilling', 'giddy', and 'stunning'

- **verbs of movement**, such as 'whisk'

3 Re-read the paragraph you have written. Are there any changes you could make to it to make it more appealing? Redraft it, making any necessary changes.

4 Now write the first drafts of the other sections of your leaflet. When you have completed your first drafts, re-read and redraft to make any improvements to your writing.

The final part of the drafting process is the writing of headings to organise the different parts of your leaflet. You can also use headings that appeal to specific audiences.

Example

If the entertainment section of your leaflet is aimed at teenagers, you might use a heading such as: **Pacy nightlife for party people**

However, if the section was aimed towards younger children, the heading could read: **Fun times for fun kids**

5 Create headings for the different sections of your leaflet, making sure they are appropriate for the audience you are targeting.

Pr Present

Layout and design

The presentation of your leaflet needs to be thought out very carefully. So far you have thought about the ways in which your leaflet should appeal to teenagers and young children in its writing style, but you now need to consider its visual appeal.

The following aspects will need to be given some thought:

- **Layout** – Where will different sections of text be positioned to their best advantage? How many pages will the leaflet have? Will it be folded? How?

- **Use of colour** – What colours will be most effective and eye-catching for different parts of text and headings? What colours could you use for the background?

- **Pictures** – Where would photographs, maps and diagrams be best placed to be eye-catching or informative?

1 Using a piece of plain paper, sketch out the layout and design of your leaflet. Show on your sketch:

- where the different sections will go
- where the headings will go
- where the pictures will go
- the sizes and colours of the various parts of your leaflet.

When you are presenting information in your leaflet, you will want to highlight the most important information or emphasise particular words or phrases that you want to draw the reader's attention to. To do this you can use different techniques:

- **bullet points** can make key information stand out

- **different fonts** can be used for different headings and pieces of text

- **font size** can be varied, with more important information presented in a larger size

- **bold**, **italics** or **underlining** can help to highlight key words or phrases.

2 Read through the final draft of your leaflet. Mark on it the fonts and font sizes that you will use for different sections and headings. Indicate the ways that you will make the key information stand out.

3 The final aspect that you will need to consider is the picture design. You need to choose pictures that will fit in with the text you have written and also appeal to the leaflet's audience of teenagers and younger children. Select the pictures that you are going to include in your leaflet. The pictures could include:

- photographs or illustrations that you have found during your research

- maps, cartoons or illustrations that you can draw yourself

- photographs that you could take.

W Writing: major task

Producing the finished leaflet

You should think about producing the final version of your leaflet using a computer, as this will help the design to look professional.

Use the following checklist to remind yourself of the important features of a leaflet.

Text	Make sure that your writing is easy for the reader to understand, as well as being interesting and appealing. Use words and phrases that get the reader involved in the leaflet. Think about the type of language you should use – emotive, persuasive, humorous?	❏
Layout	Make sure the different sections of the leaflet are arranged in a logical order. Make sure important information stands out for the reader. Leave some white space to make your leaflet easier to read.	❏
Design	Remember to use a variety of the following devices: bullet points, bold headings, different fonts and font sizes, italics, colours, etc.	❏
Pictures	The pictures you include should link to the text and help to illustrate the information you include in your writing. You should make sure that the pictures you choose appeal to the readers of the leaflet.	❏

Review of skills

Skills for learning ▶▶▶

Note-taking is a skill you need in all subjects. You have to be able to take notes from books, while listening to teachers, while watching videos and while working at a computer. Your note-taking skills will improve if you have a range of strategies for taking notes from which you can select and have thought about how best to organise and store your notes.

Reviewing note-taking strategies ▶▶▶

You won't always take notes in the same way. It is important to know which ways suit you and which ways best match the tasks you have to do. The major strategies for note-taking are listed below.

▶ Use **headings** to divide up your notes. This is useful when you have to make a lot of notes at once or when your notes are complicated.

▶ Highlight **key words** or essential information. This is a strategy to use when you are taking notes about what you are reading. Instead of reading and taking notes at the same time, read the text and highlight key words or information you want to take notes on later.

▶ Use **abbreviations** when making notes, particularly when you are writing at speed. You can use initial letters (WW2 for World War 2) or shortened forms (Xn for Christian). You could also make up your own abbreviations and add a key at the bottom of your notes.

▶ Use **note-taking grids** or tables to organise key information. This is particularly useful when you are compiling lists of points, such as arguments 'for' and 'against'.

▶ Write in **bullet-pointed phrases** rather than writing in whole sentences. This saves time when writing notes that only you will read.

▶ **Number key items** of information, perhaps in order of importance. This can be done after you have completed a set of notes. It is also a good technique to use when you brainstorm a list in random order.

▶ Represent information as a **flow chart**. This is a handy technique to use whenever you have to take notes about a process, for example, in science. You can use arrows to take the place of linking words and phrases.

Whenever you complete a major piece of work, look back at the notes you have used. Check that the note-taking strategies you have used have been appropriate to the task. Make sure that you employ a range of note-taking strategies, as the more confident you become in using different techniques, the more useful your notes will be to you.

Childhood Unit 2: Imagine

Writers have the power to appeal to their readers' imaginations and get them to **imagine** situations that they haven't considered before. Sometimes a writer will want readers to imagine the terrible suffering experienced by others because they want things to be improved. William Blake (1757–1827) was a religious poet who felt strongly that his readers should know about the wretched conditions experienced by the young, the poor, the sick and the unemployed.

In 'The Chimney-Sweeper', which you are going to read in this unit, Blake helps the reader to imagine the situation of children who worked as chimney-sweeps at the time. You are also going to look at a modern text produced by the children's charity, the NSPCC. This is a storyboard for a TV advertisement from their campaign against child abuse, which tries to give its audience an insight into the terrible abuse suffered by some children.

Pre-reading

Create two spider diagrams: one with the word 'light' in the centre and the other with the word 'dark' in the centre. Work with a partner to think of as many words as you can that are to do with lightness and darkness and complete your spider diagrams.

The Chimney-Sweeper

When my mother died I was very young,
And my father sold me while yet my tongue
Could scarcely cry 'weep, 'weep, 'weep, 'weep!
So your chimneys I sweep, and in soot I sleep.

There's little Tom Dacre, who cried when his head,
That curled like a lamb's back, was shaved: so I said,
'Hush, Tom, never mind it, for when your head's bare
You know that the soot cannot spoil your white hair.'

And so he was quiet, and that very night,
As Tom was a-sleeping he had such a sight,
That thousands of sweepers, Dick, Joe, Ned, and Jack,
Were all of them locked up in coffins of black.

And by came an angel, who had a bright key,
And he opened the coffins and set them all free;
Then down a green plain, leaping, laughing, they run,
And wash in a river and shine in the sun.

Then naked and white, all their bags left behind,
They rise upon clouds, and sport in the wind.
And the angel told Tom, if he'd be a good boy,
He'd have God for his father and never want joy.

And so Tom awoke, and we rose in the dark,
And got with our bags and our brushes to work.
Though the morning was cold, Tom was happy and warm;
So if all do their duty, they need not fear harm.

William Blake

Dictionary check

soot a black powder that is left after coal is burnt
duty work
sport play

NSPCC 'Cartoon' storyboard

NOTES

Throughout this commercial we are shown a father mentally and physically abusing his son at home. The only difference is the child is not a real child but is a cartoon child. The cartoon child recovers from each attack the real-life father makes, as cartoon characters always do. When the cartoon child is hit, for instance, a bump might appear from his head, but when he pushes it down, it disappears.

At the end of the commercial the cartoon child takes a particularly bad beating and is pushed down the stairs. Sight of him is obscured by an armchair. As we move closer we see, left on the floor, where the cartoon child lay, the body of a real child of about the same age, showing clear signs of abuse. The real child is motionless.

We are then told that ... 'Real children don't bounce back.'

Dictionary check

sfx special effects
obscured hidden
pans moves

The father enters the house. We see him go on to abuse his cartoon son in various ways.
NB: Cartoon music throughout. Also cartoon sfx when boy is being hit, etc.

For instance he hits him on the head...

He chases him out of the bedroom and throws him down the stairs ...

... where he eventually lands on the sofa.

Real children
don't bounce back

... as the camera pans round the sofa, we see a real child lying at the bottom of the stairs.
On screen appear the words:
Real children don't bounce back.

If you think a child is being abused
do something

Together we can stop child abuse. FULL STOP. ● NSPCC
For advice call our Helpline. Calls can be anonymous. 0808 800 5000
supported by Microsoft

... which change to:
If you think a child is being abused do something.
Together we can stop child abuse. FULL STOP.
For advice call our Helpline.
Calls can be anonymous.
0808 800 5000.

Tracing the main themes

1 Read 'The Chimney-Sweeper'. One way to understand what a poem is about is to retell the story of each stanza in one sentence. Copy and complete the following table.

Stanza one	*The boy narrator tells us that he was sold into chimney-sweeping when he was very young.*
Stanza two	*The reader is told about Tom Dacre, another boy chimney-sweep, who cries when his head had to be shaved, but is comforted by the narrator.*
Stanza three	
Stanza four	
Stanza five	
Stanza six	

2 In the first stanza the poet writes: 'So your chimneys I sweep, and in soot I sleep.'

   a) Who is the 'you' to whom the poet refers?

   b) What would you expect to be the attitude of this person to child chimney-sweeps?

   c) Why would the poet choose to address his poem to such a person?

3 The poet describes in detail Tom Dacre's dream.

   a) Why were the children locked in 'coffins of black'?

   b) Why would an 'angel' unlock the coffins?

   c) Why do the children 'rise upon clouds and sport in the wind'?

4 At the time Blake wrote his poem the word 'want' meant 'be in need of'. Paraphrase (translate into modern prose) the lines:

> And the angel told Tom, if he'd be a good boy,
> He'd have God for his father and never want joy.

5 Do you believe that 'Though the morning was cold, Tom was happy and warm'? Explain the reasons for your opinion.

Exploring figurative language

Poets often use **figurative language**, words that create pictures in the mind, as a way of making their readers think more deeply. Figurative language always involves a comparison, and readers often have to work hard to understand the comparisons that are being made. One of the simplest forms of figurative language is the **simile**.

Symbolism is when a word or phrase signifies something else: the word 'white' as you have seen, is often thought to symbolise the idea of innocence and light. The poem uses quite a number of **symbolic images**, and uses them as **sets of opposites**, to contrast the happy world of Tom's dream with the sad reality of his life as a chimney-sweep.

1 Identify the simile the writer uses in the poem. What idea does the writer use this simile to symbolise?

2 a) Look back at your Pre-reading activity. Now create another two spider diagrams based around the words 'light' and 'dark' by reading through the poem carefully and writing down all the words that are associated with 'lightness' and 'darkness'.

b) What similarities or repetitions are there between your lists of words from the Pre-reading activity and the words you have taken from the poem?

c) Why does Blake use the language associated with 'lightness' or 'darkness' to describe the suffering of the chimney-sweeps?

d) What do you think is the most effective line in the poem that describes the suffering of the sweeps? Give reasons.

3 Copy out and complete the table below by picking out quotations from the poem and matching them to the ideas symbolised.

Idea symbolised	Example from text	Idea symbolised	Example from text
light	'naked and white'	dark	'in soot I sleep'
play		work	
freedom		confinement	
life		death	

S Sentence level

Exploring the differences between texts

1 Both 'The Chimney-Sweeper' and the NSPCC 'Cartoon' storyboard tell stories.

    a) Why do you think writers use stories (whether in poetry or in pictures) as a way of getting their message across?

    b) What word pictures does Blake create in your mind in 'The Chimney-Sweeper'?

    c) What do you think are the most memorable words used in the NSPCC storyboard?

2 The poem is written in the first person where the chimney-sweep is telling the story from the perspective of the child. The NSPCC storyboard 'tells' the story from the point of view of someone watching what's happening.

    a) Sketch the first stanza of the poem as a storyboard for a television advertising campaign against the use of child labour.

    b) Which form is the most powerful for communicating its message – the poem or the TV commercial? Give reasons for your answer.

    c) Why might Blake (who was writing before television and radio) have chosen poetry rather than pictures or prose to communicate his ideas?

3 Re-read the following sentences from the NSPCC storyboard. Questions 3 to 6 are about this section of the storyboard.

> Real children don't bounce back.
> If you think a child is being abused do something.
> Together we can stop child abuse. FULL STOP.
> For advice call our Helpline.
> Calls can be anonymous.
> 0808 800 5000

    a) Explain what 'Real children don't bounce back' means.

    b) Count the number of words per sentence. What do you notice? Why has the writer chosen this length of sentence?

    c) Why has the writer written FULL STOP? What are the capital letters being used for here?

d) Why does the sentence ending '…we can stop child abuse' begin with the word 'together'? What would be the effect if 'together' was moved to the end of the sentence?

4 How would you describe the tone of this section of the commercial? Choose the sentence below which best matches your view. Explain the reasons for your choice, paying particular attention to the verbs used by the writer.

   a) The tone is very forceful, demanding that the audience see child abuse as their responsibility.

   b) It's helpful in tone, suggesting ways in which people can find help if they need it.

   c) The tone is neutral, simply giving information and advice.

5 The word 'can' is repeated twice in this section. Identify the sentences in which it is used.

   a) What is the meaning of each the following sentences

    • Together we can stop child abuse.

    • Together we could stop child abuse.

    • Together we will stop child abuse.

   b) Explain which you think is the most powerful sentence.

6 What is the meaning of each of the following sentences? Which wording would make you most likely to phone the helpline?

   a) Calls can be anonymous.

   b) Calls could be anonymous.

   c) Calls will be anonymous.

7 Summarise the main differences between the ways that Blake tries to get his message across to his audience and the ways in which the NSPCC tries to get its message across.

SL Speaking and listening

Exploring the text in role

You are going to work in a group of three. Imagine that the boy chimney-sweep from the poem is now grown up. He is to be interviewed on a television chat show alongside the person to whom the poem was written.

- One of you should play the interviewer. You should try to conduct the interview in a friendly way, asking questions of both guests. Try to find out what life was like at the time the poem was written and how the guests feel now about child chimney-sweeps.

- One of you should play the grown-up chimney-sweep. You should explain to the interviewer what your life was like when you were a chimney-sweep and how you feel about it now.

- One of you should play the person to whom the poem was written. You should explain what you thought about child chimney-sweeps before you read the poem and how your views about them changed.

Discuss in your group what you think the different characters would say in the interview. When you are happy with the ideas you have come up with, practise and then present the chat show to the rest of the class.

Writing to imagine

W Writing: minor task

You are now going to write a diary entry for the child chimney-sweep describing a typical day's work. Remember that diary entries are written in the first person and should reveal the writer's private thoughts and feelings about the day's events.

W Writing: major task

You are going to produce a storyboard for a television advertising campaign about an issue that you care about. This could be a campaign against cruelty to animals, the dangers of drink driving, the issue of homelessness, or your own idea,

Use the writing frame on page 23 to help you to prepare your storyboard.

What to write

Introductory statement

- Describes in detail what the storyboard will show in pictures. Follow the chronological order of the events in the advertisement.

Sequence of five slides

- Include pictures (which could be taken using a digital camera).
- For each picture, give a brief description/commentary of the action including descriptions of camera angles.
- Include additional advice in italics explaining any other effects, such as music, sound or special effects.

Final slide

- Choose a picture that conveys the message of your campaign.
- Write down the voiceover that would be spoken at the end of the advertisement including:
  - ▶ a short catchphrase summing up the message of your campaign
  - ▶ three short sentences telling the audience what they have to do and one sentence outlining the campaign's aim
  - ▶ a word or short phrase to end the advert and details of who to contact to get advice.

How to write it

Remember to use the present tense and refer to the audience using the first person plural 'we' throughout.

Link your description of what happens using connectives.

We are shown …

As we move closer …

When the …

At the end of …

Label each picture with a scene number.

Use technical abbreviations to describe the effects.

The … enters …

He runs over …

… sfx

A … soundtrack

Look for a photograph that will have a great impact on the audience, but bear in mind it should be appropriate to be seen on TV.

Stop … now

If you see …

We can …

Stop …

Call our helpline on … for …

Childhood Unit 3: Explore

Journalists often write to **explore** issues, investigating them through their writing so that their readers understand the issues better and learn more about them. You are going to read a piece of exploratory writing in which a journalist describes the findings of a survey which explores the ways in which family life has changed. At first sight you may think that this writer simply gives the plain facts, but as you read the article more closely you will begin to appreciate that facts can be presented in very different ways, depending on what the writer wants the reader to believe.

Pre-reading

Think about how decisions are taken in your family. Copy out and complete the table below. Think of six decisions that your family has taken and place a tick in whichever box best fits what happens in your family. The first box has been filled in for you, but you can replace this with your own idea if you wish.

Decisions	Children decide	Adults decide	Family decision
What to eat for dinner			

Do you think that when they were young your parents made as many decisions as you do now? Talk about this with a partner.

Children seen and clearly heard as parents consult on lifestyle choices

Modern youngsters are increasingly dominating family life, including the choice of the evening meal and the family car, according to a survey published today.

This seems to be the price parents are paying to enjoy a more open relationship with their children than they had with their own parents.

Almost three-quarters of parents in the Abbey National survey of 950 families said they were able to communicate well with their children. So well that in 65% of cases children helped to select holiday destinations, while three-quarters of parents consulted their offspring before redecorating the home.

The survey also found that nine out of ten children no longer asked what was for supper – they told their parents what to cook. And more than half had the final say on the make, model and colour of the new car.

For 84% of families organising leisure time involved negotiations between parents and children. When it came to moving house, 42% of parents sought the childrens views – especially with teenagers.

The study concluded that, in the main, family members were happy with their changing roles, with fathers particularly keen to listen to children and involve them in making decisions.

An Abbey National spokesman, Tim Harrison, said he thought the degree to which children's views and opinions were being respected was unprecedented. 'We were amazed at just how much influence children have on family life.

It is clear that the family is becoming more democratic. Respect between parents and children has become a two-way process, and we would expect that as the importance of the family grows in the 21st century so too will the importance of the children.'

Many advertisers have known for some time about child pester power. Research for the Co-operative supermarket chain suggested this month that television advertisers were exploiting this aspect of the modern family.

The Co-op, which stocks many of the products criticised in the study, said it would stop advertising unhealthy foods and drinks if they continued to be targeted at children.

A separate opinion poll of Co-op customers, by NOP, found that 73% of children pleaded with their parents to buy items they had seen publicised on television, and 77% of parents wanted such adverts banned.

Simon Bowers
From *The Guardian*

T Text level: reading

Objectivity and subjectivity

1 Read the article through carefully.

2 Scan the article to identify references to the Abbey National Survey.

    a) How many families took part in the survey?

    b) What surprised the Abbey National spokesman most about the survey?

    c) What do you understand by the phrase 'Respect for the family has become a two-way process'? Do you think this is true in your own and your friends' families?

3 Re-read closely the first three paragraphs. What does the writer mean when he writes of the price parents are paying? What word in the first paragraph suggests that the writer might not altogether like the recent changes in family life?

4 What examples does the writer give of parents and children being able to communicate well? How does this compare with your experiences in your own family? Look back to the Pre-reading activity to help you with this question.

5 Re-read the paragraph beginning 'It is clear that the family is becoming more democratic.' What reasons can you think of for the importance of the family growing in the 21st century? Can you think of any reasons for the family becoming less important rather than more important in the future?

6 Read the last three paragraphs closely. Sum up in a sentence what this part of the article is about.

7 The Co-op survey found that 77% of parents would like television advertisements which are aimed at children to be banned. Do you think that the writer of the article would agree? Back up your argument by writing down the words or phrases which show what the writer thinks of television advertising aimed at children.

Main and subordinate clauses

It is very important to learn vocabulary that allows you to describe what language itself is doing. You are now going to revise three more key words to do with sentences: **complex sentence**, **main clause** and **subordinate clause**.

1 a) Read the following sentence taken from the newspaper article:

Modern youngsters are increasingly dominating family life, including the choice of the evening meal and the family car, according to a survey published today.

b) Imagine that the words between the commas aren't there. Read the sentence aloud. Does it still make sense?

2 a) Read the next sentence taken from the newspaper article:

The Co-op, which stocks many of the products criticised in the study, said it would stop advertising unhealthy foods and drinks if they continued to be targeted at children.

b) Which part of the sentence could you remove and still leave the sentence making sense?

The sentences you have just read are called **complex sentences**. These are sentences which consist of a **main clause** and one or more **subordinate clauses**.

Example

Subordinate clause

Modern youngsters are increasingly dominating family life, including the choice of the evening meal and the family car, <u>according to a survey published today.</u>

Subordinate clause

The Co-op, <u>which stocks many of the products criticised in the study,</u> said it would stop advertising unhealthy foods and drinks <u>if they continued to be targeted at children</u>.

Subordinate clause

3 Write down a sentence containing a main and a subordinate clause or clauses exploring what you think about the following topics:

a) Advertisers who target young children
b) Parents who give in to their childrens demands
c) Parents who want TV adverts aimed at young children banned.

Subordinate means 'of less importance'. A subordinate clause is less important than the main clause because you can take it out and the sentence will still make sense. Often you will find the writer has put the subordinate clause inside commas, marking it off from the main clause. This is important because the job of the subordinate clause is to add information to the main clause.

S Sentence level

Paragraphing and cohesion

1 Re-read the first four paragraphs of the newspaper article.

The writer has linked together the paragraphs very carefully. There are lots of different ways of doing this and the more ways you know the more interesting your own writing will become. Three ways of linking paragraphs are:

▶ Using **pronouns** that refer back to the previous paragraph, such as 'he', 'she', 'it', 'this' and 'that'.

▶ Repeating words you have used before.

▶ Using connecting words, such as 'also', 'as well', 'in addition', 'either' and 'too'. These words are called **adverbials**.

2 Re-read paragraph two closely. What word (a pronoun) only makes sense if you link it back to the first paragraph?

3 Re-read paragraph three. What four words (nouns) are used in this paragraph that have been used in the previous two paragraphs?

4 Re-read paragraph four. What adverbial is used here to connect this paragraph to the one before?

Preparing a speech

You are going to work in a group of four to prepare a brief speech on the subject 'Young people have too much freedom today'. In your group take ten minutes to discuss the subject and to decide whether the group agrees or disagrees. Then:

▶ Decide how you are going to introduce your speech. In your introduction you should make it clear what the group's views are on the subject and how you are going to discuss it.

▶ Think of an example that backs up your group's point of view. This could be an incident from your own personal experience which proves that young people do or don't have too much freedom.

▶ Think of a more general example that backs up your group's point of view. You could refer to incidents in the news or things that you have read.

▶ Think of a conclusion that sums up what your group has said about the subject.

Each member of the group should write up one part of the speech, using no more than four sentences. Remember you are going to read aloud what you have written to the rest of the class. Work as a group to write sentences that link each part of the speech together. Remember what you have learned about finding interesting ways to do this.

When you are happy with the speech, read it out to the rest of the class. Each member of the group should read out part of the speech.

Writing to explore

W (Writing: minor task)

Write up the speech that your group made to the class. Before you begin to write, you should re-read the speech and decide whether you want to change or add any details.

Make any necessary changes that you think would have made the speech work better and then write up your revised speech.

W (Writing: major task)

The article you have just read, exploring how children are taking a greater part in making family decisions, could have been written in an entirely different way by another writer with a different viewpoint.

Using the information in the article, write a 200-word article, suitable for publication in a newspaper, written from the viewpoint of a child who has been horrified to find out that parents are consulted at all.

Begin by collecting the information you will need from the article, using the planning frame opposite to help you. Fill in the left-hand column first with as many facts as you can find from the survey. Then fill in the right-hand column, trying to think how each fact might look from the viewpoint of a child who believes that children have equal rights with parents. You may use the examples provided here or choose your own.

Try to find five or six facts to put in the planning frame. Remember to use the whole article to find information, not just the first few paragraphs.

Planning frame

Facts from the survey	Facts written from the child's point of view
1 Three quarters of parents in the survey said they were able to communicate well with their children.	1 A quarter of all parents cannot communicate with their children.
2 In 65% of families children are consulted about holiday destinations.	2 A third of all children are not even consulted about where they are going to go on holiday.
3	3
4	4

When you have completed your planning you can begin to draft your newspaper article. Use the writing frame below to help you.

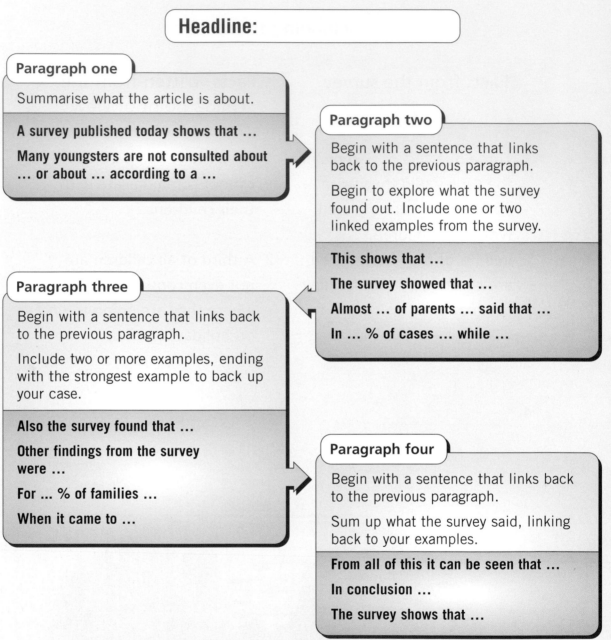

Headline:

Paragraph one

Summarise what the article is about.

A survey published today shows that …

Many youngsters are not consulted about … or about … according to a …

Paragraph two

Begin with a sentence that links back to the previous paragraph.

Begin to explore what the survey found out. Include one or two linked examples from the survey.

This shows that …

The survey showed that …

Almost … of parents … said that …

In … % of cases … while …

Paragraph three

Begin with a sentence that links back to the previous paragraph.

Include two or more examples, ending with the strongest example to back up your case.

Also the survey found that …

Other findings from the survey were …

For … % of families …

When it came to …

Paragraph four

Begin with a sentence that links back to the previous paragraph.

Sum up what the survey said, linking back to your examples.

From all of this it can be seen that …

In conclusion …

The survey shows that …

Help box

1 Remember to use **complex sentences** (including one or more **subordinate clauses**) in order to pack more information into your article.

2 Try to use **adverbials** to link your paragraphs together.

Childhood Unit 4: Entertain

Writers use many techniques to make their writing **entertaining**. Exaggeration and repetition are two such techniques and have been used in this extract from Frank McCourt's best selling autobiography, *Angela's Ashes*, set in 1930s Ireland. Frank's grandmother has taken in a new lodger called Bill Galvin and a reluctant Frank has been given the job (for which he is to be paid sixpence a week) of taking Bill a cooked dinner every day at his place of work.

Before you read, think back to a time when you did something wrong and had to make up an excuse to get yourself out of trouble. Tell your story to a partner and be prepared to tell your partner's story to the rest of the class. Make notes, as you will revisit this activity later in the unit.

Angela's Ashes

Every morning Grandma cooks Bill's dinner and takes it to him at the lime kiln. Mam wonders why he can't take it with him in the morning and Grandma says, Do you expect me to get up at dawn and boil cabbage and pig's toes for his lordship to take in his dinner can?

Mam tells her, In another week school will be over and if you give Frank sixpence a week he'll surely be glad to take Bill Galvin his dinner.

I don't want to go to Grandma's every day. I don't want to take Bill Galvin his dinner all the way down the Dock Road, but Mam says that's sixpence we could use and if I don't do it I'm going nowhere else.

You're staying in the house, she says. You're not playing with your pals.

Grandma warns me to take the dinner can directly and not be meandering, looking this way and that, kicking canisters and ruining the toes of my shoes. This dinner is hot and that's the way Bill Galvin wants it.

There's a lovely smell from the dinner can, boiled bacon and cabbage and two big floury white potatoes. Surely he won't notice if I try half a potato. He won't complain to Grandma because he hardly ever talks outside of a snuffle or two.

It's better if I eat the other half potato so that he won't be asking why he got a half. I might as well try the bacon and cabbage too and if I eat the other potato he'll surely think she didn't send one at all.

The second potato melts in my mouth and I'll have to try another bit of cabbage, another morsel of bacon. There isn't much left now and he'll be very suspicious so I might as well finish off the rest.

What am I going to do now? Grandma will destroy me, Mam will keep me in for a year. Bill Galvin will bury me in lime. I'll tell him I was attacked by a dog on the Dock Road and he ate the whole dinner and I'm lucky I escaped without being eaten myself.

Oh, is that so? says Bill Galvin. And what's that bit of cabbage hanging on your gansey? Did the dog lick you wit his cabbagey gob? Go home and tell your grandmother you ate me whole dinner and I'm falling down with the hunger here in this lime kiln.

She'll kill me.

Tell her don't kill you till she sends me some class of a dinner and if you don't go to her now and get me a dinner I'll kill you and throw your body into the lime there and there won't be much left for your mother to moan over.

Grandma says, What are you doin' back with that can? He could bring that back by himself.

He wants more dinner.

What do you mean more dinner? Jesus above, is it a hole he has in his leg?

He's falling down with the hunger below in the lime kiln.

Is it coddin' me you are?

He says send him any class of a dinner.

I will not. I sent him his dinner.

He didn't get it.

He didn't? Why not?

I ate it.

What?

I was hungry and I tasted it and I couldn't stop.

Jesus, Mary and holy St. Joseph.

She gives me a clout on the head that brings tears to my eyes. She screams at me like a banshee and jumps around the kitchen and threatens to drag me to the priest, the bishop, the Pope himself if he lived around the corner. She cuts bread and waves the knife at me and makes sandwiches of brawn and cold potatoes.

Take these sandwiches to Bill Galvin and if you even look cross-eyed at them I'll skin your hide.

Of course she runs to Mam and they agree the only way I can make up for my terrible sin is to deliver Bill Galvin's dinner for a fortnight without pay. I'm to bring back the can every day and that means I have to sit watching him stuff the food into his gob and he's not one that would ever ask you if you had a mouth in your head.

Every day I take the can back Grandma makes me kneel to the statue of the Sacred Heart and tell Him I'm sorry and all this over Bill Galvin, a Protestant.

From *Angela's Ashes* by Frank McCourt

T Text level: reading

Investigating entertaining texts

1 What title would you give to the extract? It must let the reader know that it's going to be an entertaining read.

2 The author doesn't tell us information about his family directly, but we know a lot about them from what they say and do. What three pieces of evidence can you find in the text to suggest that this is:

   a) a very poor family?
   b) a religious family?
   c) a close family?

3 Frank convinces himself that he can get away with eating Bill's dinner. What are his reasons for thinking this?

4 How can the reader tell that Grandma does not altogether like Bill Galvin?

5 Frank thinks of three punishments he might face.

   a) What are these punishments?
   b) What does actually happen to him?
   c) Do these punishments in your view fit his 'crime'?

6 The writer uses two particular writing techniques to make the story he is telling amusing. Find examples in the extract of both of the following techniques, using quotations to back up your answers.

   a) The use of **exaggeration**, such as 'She'll kill me.'
   b) The use of **repetition**, such as 'Grandma will destroy me, Mam will keep me in for a year, Bill Galvin will bury me in lime.' Remember that repeated words or phrases don't have to be exactly next to each other.

Standard English and other dialects

Standard English is the variety of English normally used in writing and is the most widely understood form of English. You will hear speakers of standard English all over the English-speaking world. Standard English is spoken or written according to the standard rules of usage of grammar, spelling and vocabulary.

> Example
>
> Standard English: *I'm not doing anything.*
>
> Non-standard English: *I ain't doing nothing.*

Dialects are forms of non-standard English. We call the variety of English used in one area a dialect. It is easy to distinguish between a dialect and standard English because a dialect uses different vocabulary (individual words and phrases) and grammar (the way sentences are constructed). A dialect can show you where somebody comes from, whether it's a particular country, district or city. This is different from a person's **accent**, which is only a matter of pronunciation, the way language is spoken. Both dialect and standard English can be spoken in a variety of different accents.

> Example
>
> *The word 'gansey' and the sentence construction 'Is it coddin' me you are?' are examples of an Irish dialect.*

1 Copy and complete the grid below by providing standard English equivalents for the dialect words used in the extract you have read.

Dialect word	Standard English equivalent
Mam	
gansey	
gob	
wit	
coddin'	
banshee	

2 Each of the following sentences i) to iii) uses dialect grammar and is constructed differently to sentences using standard English. Read them and answer questions a) to c) about them below.

   i) It's better if I eat the other half potato so that he won't be asking why he got a half.

   ii) I'm falling down with the hunger here in this lime kiln.

   iii) Is it coddin' me you are?

   a) Which sentence uses an auxiliary verb ('be' or 'have') to make the future tense when standard English does not use one?

   b) Which sentence includes 'a', 'an' or 'the' before the noun when standard English would leave it out?

   c) Find another example of dialect grammar in the extract and explain how it is different from standard English.

3 The writer of *Angela's Ashes* has decided to use non-standard punctuation, for example, leaving out the conventional punctuation of speech. Rewrite the conversation between Bill Galvin and Frank, reprinted below, into spoken standard English, using conventional speech punctuation for direct speech.

> Oh, is that so? says Bill Galvin. And what's that bit of cabbage hanging on your gansey? Did the dog lick you wit his cabbagey gob? Go home and tell your grandmother you ate me whole dinner and I'm falling down with the hunger here in this lime kiln.
> She'll kill me.
> Tell her don't kill you till she sends me some class of a dinner and if you don't go to her now and get me a dinner I'll kill you and throw your body into the lime there and there won't be much left for your mother to moan over.

4 What impact has leaving out conventional speech punctuation had? Why do you think the writer might have done this?

Explore the effectiveness of changes in tense

Frank McCourt has made his writing seem more real and immediate by writing in the **present tense**, as if it is happening now. It makes us feel that what is being recounted is happening before our very eyes, rather like watching a commentary on the action in a film or a play. The present tense verbs in the following example have been underlined.

> Example
>
> She _screams_ at me like a banshee and _jumps_ around the kitchen and _threatens_ to drag me to the priest, the bishop, the Pope himself …

Tense refers to the way verbs are used to signal time. All of the verbs in the table below are **regular verbs**. Regular verbs form their present tense by adding '-s' to the base form of the verb when in the third person (he, she, it) and form their past tense by adding '-ed' to the base form of the verb.

Base form verb	Present tense	Past tense
scream	screams	screamed
jump	jumps	jumped
threaten	threatens	threatened

1 Rewrite the following paragraph that is taken from the text by transforming the present tense verbs into the past tense.

She gives me a clout on the head that brings tears to my eyes. She screams at me like a banshee and jumps around the kitchen and threatens to drag me to the priest, the bishop, the Pope himself if he lived around the corner. She cuts bread and waves the knife at me and makes sandwiches of brawn and cold potatoes.

2 Look again at your rewritten paragraph. Comment on the effect that your changes have had on the text.

3 **a)** Write a short commentary of a sporting moment as if you are commentator on the radio.

b) Then write a paragraph in an newspaper report from the next day, reporting the same sporting moment.

c) Re-read your two pieces. What differences can you see between the two pieces? What effect do the differences create?

SL Speaking and listening

Retelling an anecdote

Look back at the notes you made for the Pre-reading activity on page 33. You are now going to retell the story of a time when your partner did something wrong to the rest of the class. You will need to make the retelling of this incident as entertaining as possible.

First of all, check that you have found out all the information you need about the incident from your partner and then organise the information in a way that will help you to retell the story.

You need to consider the ways in which you can make your retelling of the story as entertaining as possible. Think about:

- repeating any particularly funny phrases or details to emphasise them for the audience

- exaggerating any important details, such as the way you describe your partner's excuse

- including direct speech to show what your partner said and what people said to him or her at the time

- retelling your story using the present tense to heighten the impact of the story on your audience, by making it sound as if it is happening as they are listening.

When you have practised your retelling using some of these techniques, retell the story to your partner. Ask him or her to point out any parts of the story that you could make more entertaining. Your partner might want you to focus on a particular part of the story in more detail or could remind you of the exact words used at the time.

When you have listened to your partner's advice and made any necessary changes, present the retelling to the rest of the class.

Writing to entertain

 **W** (Writing: minor task)

Write up the story of the time when your partner did something wrong and made up an excuse to try to get out of trouble. Use the notes that you made for the Speaking and listening activity on page 39 to help you with your first draft of writing. You should retell the story using 250 words or fewer.

You should make sure that you include the techniques you used in the Speaking and listening activity to make your writing as entertaining as possible.

W (Writing: major task)

You are now going to write an entertaining story that continues the adventures of Frank from *Angela's Ashes*. To do this you need to think about what could happen after the extract finishes.

The extract ends with Frank being made to deliver Bill Galvin's dinner for a fortnight without pay, as well as having to bring back the can and ask for forgiveness in front of a religious statue every day.

Imagine that Frank decides to get his revenge on Bill Galvin for getting him into trouble with his Grandma. Think about how Frank could decide to do this and what the consequences of his actions would be. Use the planning frame opposite to help you to organise your ideas.

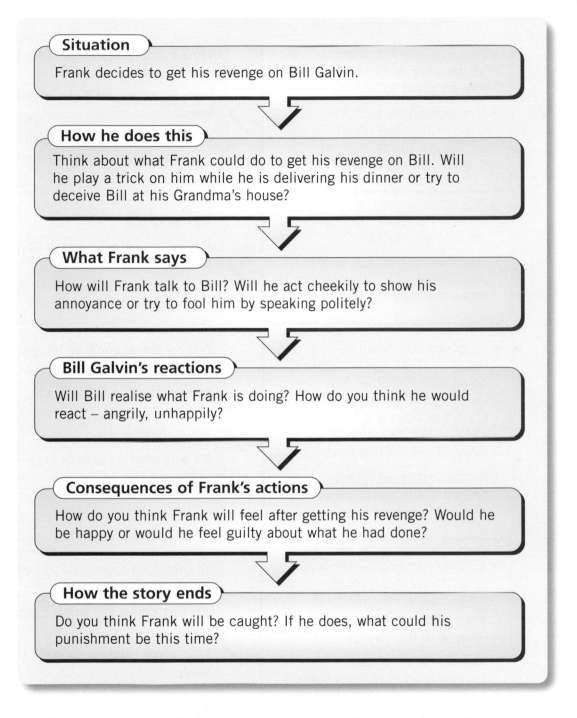

Situation

Frank decides to get his revenge on Bill Galvin.

How he does this

Think about what Frank could do to get his revenge on Bill. Will he play a trick on him while he is delivering his dinner or try to deceive Bill at his Grandma's house?

What Frank says

How will Frank talk to Bill? Will he act cheekily to show his annoyance or try to fool him by speaking politely?

Bill Galvin's reactions

Will Bill realise what Frank is doing? How do you think he would react – angrily, unhappily?

Consequences of Frank's actions

How do you think Frank will feel after getting his revenge? Would he be happy or would he feel guilty about what he had done?

How the story ends

Do you think Frank will be caught? If he does, what could his punishment be this time?

When you have worked out the plot of your story, use the writing frame on page 42 to help you with the first draft of your writing.

What to write

- Describe why Frank wants to get his revenge on Bill Galvin and how he plans to do this.
- Use techniques such as exaggeration and repetition to emphasise the strength of Frank's feelings.

- Describe the way Frank puts his plan into action.
- Try to include dialect words and sentence constructions to make the story sound realistic.

- Include a conversation between Frank and Bill Galvin. Think about whether Bill Galvin would be suspicious of Frank's actions and the excuses that Frank could use to avoid getting into trouble.
- Remember to set direct speech out in the same way as it is in the extract.

- End your story on a humorous note. Think about whether it will be funnier for the reader if Frank gets caught or if he gets away with his revenge.
- Use the techniques of exaggeration or repetition again to show how Frank feels at the end of the story.

Sentence starters

Every morning this week I take Bill Galvin's dinner …

Every time I just sit there watching him …

When I get him back he'll wish …

So I try to …

If Bill finds out what I've done he'll …

Is it my dinner you'll be bringing there? says Bill. You better …

I'm just about to open my gob when …

What's this?

It's only what my Grandma told me to bring. She said …

Of course my Grandma's still going to clout me when …

But just seeing Bill Galvin's face when …

I fall about laughing so much I think …

Help box

1 Remember to make your writing seem more immediate and real by writing in the **present tense**.

Skills for writing ▶▶▶

Proof reading is the process of re-reading your written work in order to find and correct mistakes. Being able to proof read quickly and accurately is a skill that will help improve your writing in all subjects. It is particularly useful to be able to proof read quickly in tests.

You will become a much more accurate proof reader if:

▶ you know what your most common **spelling mistakes** are

▶ you know what **punctuation errors** to look for in your own writing

▶ you know what **grammatical errors** you are most likely to make

▶ you practise often to improve your speed and accuracy.

Proof reading journal ▶▶▶

Find some examples of your own writing over the last year. Work with a partner and look at each person's work in turn. Write down examples of the following:

a) your three most common spelling errors. Look for patterns – do you always double the 'l' at the end of words such as 'beautiful'? Perhaps you forget to double the consonant in words such as 'stopped' or 'running'?

b) the three errors of punctuation you have made most often. Do you get confused with apostrophes of possession? Do you always punctuate direct speech correctly?

c) the three grammatical rules you find most difficult. Perhaps you start a story writing in the third person and end up writing in the first person or perhaps you change tense half way through.

When you have done this, write out a checklist of the errors you need to look for when you are proof reading your own work. Copy out and complete the table below, which has an example for you to follow.

What I do wrong	Example of this from my work	Corrected version
I forget capital letters at the start of direct speech.	*"run!" shouted David.*	*"Run!" shouted David.*

Keep this table and use it when you are proof reading your own writing. You will find that you need to update it, because your writing will keep improving and you will make fewer errors.

We rely on writing that gives **information** about how to do things. It is important to be able to find key information without reading the whole piece so the way in which the material is presented is almost as important as the content because it has to be accessible to the reader.

The text you are going to look at is a news supplement feature which introduces the idea of a 'Buy Nothing Day' on which absolutely nothing is bought, as a protest against consumer culture. You are going to study how the organisational features in the text work together to give you, the reader, a great deal of information.

Pre-reading

Logos play an important part in shopping. Sketch your two favourite designer logos. Work with a friend to decide what the logo is trying to tell you about the product.

A job for consumers: try to buy nothing

November 24 is Buy Nothing Day. Founded by the Canadian artist Ted Dave, the concept began in 1993. Today, Buy Nothing Day is held in more than 30 countries. The idea is that you go the whole day without buying a thing – not a pint of milk, not even a bus ticket.

Every year in Britain we use seven billion plastic carrier bags, more than 300 for every household. They carry our groceries, our magazines, our new trainers. Plastic bags are one of the many by-products of our consumer society.

At a time when the prime minister is encouraging us all to spend, spend, spend in an effort to stave off recession, Ted Dave and other supporters of Buy Nothing Day say that their argument is not with our love of buying things, but with what we buy.

In England and Wales alone, 400 million tonnes of waste are produced every year. In one week alone, Britain produces enough waste to fill Wembley Stadium. We use more than six billion glass bottles and jars annually, and our demand for paper and cardboard requires a forest the size of Wales every year. Yet a mere 8% of our rubbish is recycled – instead, 83% goes into landfill sites.

Nearly everything we buy comes packaged and branded to perfection, swathed in tissue paper, cellophane, cardboard, plastic and padding. Last Christmas alone we chucked out 270,000 tonnes of packaging. Our society encourages us not to re-use or recycle, but to buy afresh. Instead of mending an item, we throw it away and buy a new one. Constantly changing fashions mean that we see our clothes as short-term investments; the latest trends can be bought cheaply and easily on the high street.

But these disposable fashions come at a cost. In order to supply these items at such low prices, companies rely on the labour of developing countries. In these nations there are rarely labour regulations to govern and protect

Early starts in many countries, even young children work

workers' rights. Many slave away in 'sweatshops', working long hours in poor conditions for very little reward.

It is another example of the dominance of the Haves over the Have-Nots, in a world where 20% of the population is gobbling over 80% of the earth's natural resources.

Buy Nothing Day encourages us not only to question our thirst for brands, but also to think about how they are made and the consequences of their production. The west's desire for luxury goods drains not only the already impoverished developing countries, but also harms the environment, with the destruction of wildlife and the dumping of waste products.

Laura Barton
From *The Guardian*

> **Did you know?**
> In Canada and the U.S, Buy Nothing Day falls a day earlier, on November 23, the day following Thanksgiving Day. In Europe it is the Saturday after Thanksgiving, because Saturday is traditionally the popular day for shopping.

Using a range of reading strategies

1 Scan the article before you read it. Sections of the text have been presented in very different ways, such as in bold print.

a) How many different layouts of text can you identify?
b) Why do you think the editor of the newspaper used these different layouts for different parts of the article?

2 Now look at the photograph and its caption.

a) What does it suggest the article might be about?
b) How might this link in with the headline?

3 Decide how you are going to read the article. Write down which of the following ways of reading it matches your reading plan.

▶ Read the whole article from start to finish.

▶ Read the marked-off section first.

▶ Read the article and cross-refer to the marked-off section.

▶ Read the article and ignore the marked-off section, you will read this later if you need to.

▶ Read in another way not listed here. Describe briefly your plan to read the article.

4 Read the article closely, using your reading plan. What is 'Buy Nothing Day' and how long has it existed? Did your reading plan help you to find this information quickly?

5 Look again at the first paragraph.

a) What does the writer mean when she writes that 'Plastic bags are one of the many by-products of our consumer society'?
b) Name another by-product.

6 In what two ways do you think our society encourages us '… not to re-use or recycle, but to buy afresh'?

7 Re-read the final paragraph. What are the three consequences that the writer describes as being a result of the 'west's desire for luxury goods'?

Personal pronouns

Pronouns are words that can replace a noun. One group of pronouns are known as **personal pronouns** and these include words such as 'I', 'you', 'he', 'she', 'it', 'we' and 'they'. Using pronouns is very useful as it means that writers can avoid having to use the same noun repeatedly. The use of personal pronouns can also help the writer to develop a relationship with the reader by creating a familiar tone.

1 Re-read the first four paragraphs of the article. Count how many times the writer uses each of the personal pronouns: 'we', 'us' and 'our', in these four paragraphs. Write down your answer.

2 Rewrite one of the first four paragraphs, but change the pronouns used by:

- changing 'we' to 'they'
- changing 'our' to 'their'
- changing 'us' to 'them'.

3 Read through the paragraph you have just rewritten.

  a) How has changing the pronouns altered the meaning of the paragraph?
  b) What point do you think the writer is making by using 'we', 'us' and 'you'?

Topic sentences and linking ideas

When writing non-fiction, writers usually begin paragraphs by stating a key idea, which they then go on to develop. This prepares the reader for what the paragraph is going to be about. This first sentence is often known as a **topic sentence**. Writers also pay close attention to the order in which they arrange the sentences that follow the topic sentence in paragraphs.

A common pattern of sentence organisation used in information texts is that of a topic sentence, followed by examples given in the body of the paragraph and a concluding sentence that introduces a new idea and links to the next paragraph.

Example

In England and Wales alone, 400 million tonnes of waste are produced every year. — Topic sentence introducing the main idea in the paragraph

In one week alone Britain produces enough waste to fill Wembley Stadium. — Example giving evidence to back up the main point

We use more than six billion glass bottles and jars annually, and our demand for paper and cardboard requires a forest the size of Wales every year. — Another example giving evidence to back up the main point

Yet a mere 8% of our rubbish is recycled – instead, 83% goes into landfill sites. — New point moving the argument forward, usually linking up with the idea in next paragraph

1 Identify another paragraph from the article which uses a similar structure to the above example. Copy it out and annotate it in the same way.

The final paragraph of the newspaper article shows a second way of organising ideas in paragraphs. The two main ideas in the paragraph are linked together by the **connecting phrases** 'not only' and 'but also'.

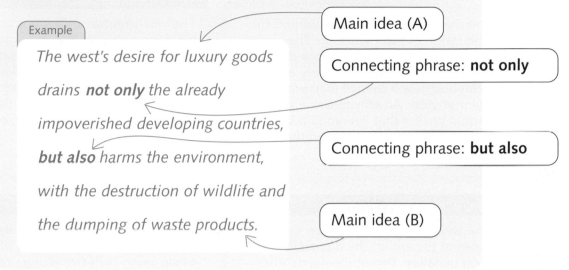

Example

The west's desire for luxury goods drains **not only** the already impoverished developing countries, **but also** harms the environment, with the destruction of wildlife and the dumping of waste products.

Main idea (A)

Connecting phrase: **not only**

Connecting phrase: **but also**

Main idea (B)

2 Identify another paragraph in the article that uses the same structure to link two main ideas.

SL Speaking and listening

Taking different roles in a discussion

You are going to discuss the question of products that are targeted at young people. This is an important issue because lots of companies deliberately use logos and designer labels to sell their products, aiming their advertising at teenagers who often do not have a lot of money to spend.

These are the questions you are going to discuss:

a) Do you ever buy products with designer labels or logos?
b) How would you choose between a product with a designer label and a cheaper product without one?
c) Why are designer labels and logos important to young people?
d) If you could abolish all designer labels, would you do so? Give reasons for your answer.

You are going to work in a group of ten. You will need to nominate a chairperson, a vice-chairperson, a scribe, a spokesperson and an observer. The rest of the group will act as team members.

The chairperson

The chairperson's job is to start off the discussion of each question. The chairperson should make sure that each question is discussed properly and that everyone gets a chance to express their point of view. An effective chairperson should ensure that everyone takes part in the discussion and remind the group of the time they have left.

The vice-chairperson

The vice-chairperson's job is to sum up what the group thinks about each question in turn. The vice-chairperson should check carefully to make sure that he or she has understood exactly what the group thinks and if there is more than one point of view, present the different opinions clearly.

The scribe

The scribe's job is to write up brief notes at the end of the discussion of each question. The scribe needs to make sure that the main points of the discussion are noted down. The notes must be neat and legible.

The spokesperson

The spokesperson's job is to explain the group's views to the rest of the class, using both the scribe's notes and their own thoughts to communicate clearly what the group felt about each issue. An effective spokesperson should speak in a clear and confident way.

Team members

The remainder of the group are team members. Their job is to contribute to the discussion, making their points clearly and referring to examples drawn from their personal experience or from their knowledge of the issue. An effective team member will stay focussed on the question being discussed.

The observer

The observer's job is to keeps notes on how each person carried out their task. The observer should think about the different skills needed by each member of the group and note down any examples of effective behaviour. At the end of the activity the observer should give the group a total score out of ten for its performance.

In your group, you should spend:

- twenty minutes discussing the questions, with the observer and the scribe making notes
- five minutes at the end of the discussion making sure the spokesperson has the necessary information.

The spokesperson should then present the team's views to the rest of the class, using the scribe's notes to help. After this, the observer should give the team feedback on their discussion and presentation.

Writing to inform

W Writing: minor task

Think back to the Pre-reading task where you identified and drew two existing product logos. You are now going to design your own logo for a product that hasn't got one already. Remember that the purpose of a logo is to say something about the product. It should catch your attention and be instantly recognisable.

When you have designed your logo, you should write a four-paragraph e-mail to the managing director of the company that produces the product. You should tell him or her:

- what the product is and where the logo will appear on it
- what each part of the logo means and what it tells you about the product
- who the logo will appeal to.

W Writing: major task

You are going to create a leaflet to promote and gain support for Buy Nothing Day in your school. You will need to include information about:

- what Buy Nothing Day is
- the reasons for it
- how to participate in it at home and at school
- where to apply for more information.

The leaflet should be no more than 300 words long. It should be attractively presented and easy to read and to follow. Use the writing frame on the next page to help you.

What is Buy Nothing Day?	Why do we need Buy Nothing Day?
• Start each paragraph with a topic sentence. • Give two examples to back up the main idea. • End your paragraph with a new point that links to the next page of your leaflet.	• Compare and contrast things in the past with how they are today. • Use the connecting phrases 'not only ... but also' to link together the main ideas in a paragraph.
Buy Nothing Day is ... **For one day people all over the world ...** **One way Buy Nothing Day works is ...** **This is important because ...**	**We used to buy things without thinking ...** **Nowadays we realise that developing countries ...** **Buy Nothing Day helps not only ... but also ...**

What to do at home and at school if you want to join in	How to get more information
• Give a bulleted list of suggestions for activities in and out of school to support Buy Nothing Day.	• Give the name of the website where further information is available. Explain what information is available there. Include a contact telephone number and postal address.
In school • **Bring packed lunches in a washable sandwich box** • **Out of school** •	**You will find out more at: www. ...** **This website includes information about ...** **For an information pack call ... or write to ...**

Help box

1. You may wish to use **headings**, **subheadings** and **separate sections of text**, as well as **different font sizes and types**, to make the information you are presenting easy to read and to understand.

2. You could also include **photographs** and **illustrations** to support the information in the text of the leaflet.

Environment

An **explanation** text explains the processes of how and why something happens or the way something works. Sometimes it combines both of these. The writer of an explanation text needs to consider how much knowledge and experience the audience already has of the subject being explained.

The explanation text you are about to read is from an educational website called 'Waste Watch – Schools and Kids'. It is about how recycling can help the environment and explains how a worm composter can be made. The process of worm composting entails feeding compost worms with kitchen waste so that garden compost is ultimately produced.

Pre-reading

Read the following short 'nonsense' text. Then write down four ways in which you can recognise that this is a text giving instructions, without needing to understand what it is saying.

> ### How to snazzle a romby-buster
>
> Romby-bustering is blasterfastic and fredicious to do.
> You keer:
> a brin, a bastic, two spudnics and a frud. (The frud needs to be quellant.)
>
> ### Snazzling the romby-buster
>
> Won dollot these derects to snazzle your romby-buster:
> * wasp the brin
> * pour frimple into bastic and shallop
> * heat the frud to boiling point
> * iron the quallant frud until smoothly.
>
> ZAMPFER! Quallant fruds can squallop! Wear brusterblubs on your hands.

Waste watch – schools and kids

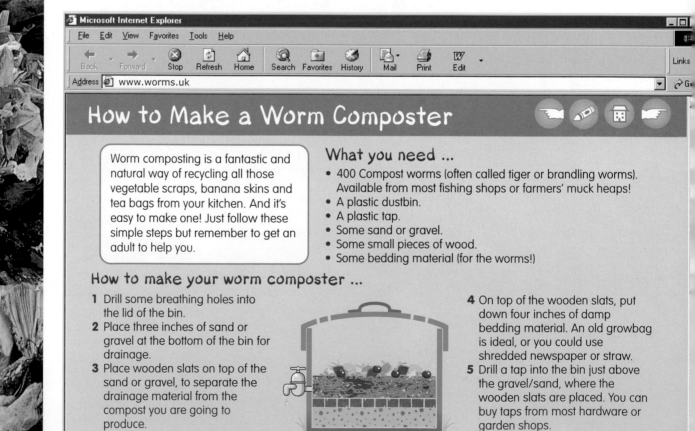

Microsoft Internet Explorer

File   Edit   View   Favorites   Tools   Help

Back   Forward   Stop   Refresh   Home   Search   Favorites   History   Mail   Print   Edit   Links

Address www.worms.uk

How to Make a Worm Composter

Worm composting is a fantastic and natural way of recycling all those vegetable scraps, banana skins and tea bags from your kitchen. And it's easy to make one! Just follow these simple steps but remember to get an adult to help you.

What you need ...

* 400 Compost worms (often called tiger or brandling worms). Available from most fishing shops or farmers' muck heaps!
* A plastic dustbin.
* A plastic tap.
* Some sand or gravel.
* Some small pieces of wood.
* Some bedding material (for the worms!)

How to make your worm composter ...

1 Drill some breathing holes into the lid of the bin.
2 Place three inches of sand or gravel at the bottom of the bin for drainage.
3 Place wooden slats on top of the sand or gravel, to separate the drainage material from the compost you are going to produce.

4 On top of the wooden slats, put down four inches of damp bedding material. An old growbag is ideal, or you could use shredded newspaper or straw.
5 Drill a tap into the bin just above the gravel/sand, where the wooden slats are placed. You can buy taps from most hardware or garden shops.

Once you have built your wormery, dig a small hollow in the bedding material and place the worms inside. Then you can start adding your food scraps. Always make sure the scraps are chopped up well. There are two main ways of feeding the worms:

- Place the food scraps on the surface of the bedding in a layer (up to 2 inches deep), but don't cover the whole surface as the worms need a small area to escape if conditions get unpleasant.

- Alternatively you can bury small batches of food scraps in the bedding, around the bin. Some people prefer this way as they feel the waste is covered up and is out of the way of flies.

With both methods you need to keep a thick sheet of wet newspapers over the surface to keep the light out and moisture in. Only add more food when the worms have finished their last lot. The speed the food is processed will depend on the number of worms, the time of year and the type of food added.

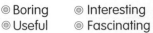

Worms Like

Egg shells (Worms need calcium and egg shells are an excellent way of supplying this and keeping the bin from getting too acidic.)
Coffee grounds and tea bags
Cereals
Baked Beans
Fruit
Bread
Cow/horse manure
Rice or pasta
Vegetable peelings

Worms Don't Like

Meat and fish (Worms will eat these but they are best avoided as they tend to putrify and attract rats and flies.)
Grass in any quantity (heats up and gives off ammonia, both of which will kill worms)
Weed seeds
Diseased plant material
Cat/dog faeces (these contain human parasites)

CAUTION ...
Never overfeed the wormery. The food will just rot, upsetting the worms and making nasty smells!

You can keep your worm bin outside but in winter the worms will be warmer (and hungrier) if you keep inside a garage or shed.

After a few weeks you should be able to collect some liquid through the tap which you can use as a liquid to feed for your plants. After a few months you can empty the bin, put the worms back and start again! And of course you'll have some excellent compost which the worms will have left behind to help everything grow better in the garden.

Your Problems Solved

I have lots of tiny flies in my worm bin – is this a health risk?
No. These are probably fruit flies, which commonly occur on rotting fruit and vegetables. A tight fitting lid will help exclude them. Also, if you bury the vegetable waste as you add it, or keep it covered with damp newspaper, they are less likely to be a problem. Flies do not harm the compost, although they can be irritating and offensive to some people.

I opened my worm bin to find hundreds of worms around the lid – why?
Either they have run out of food or the conditions in the bin have become unsuitable for them. Worms hate waterlogged, acidic compost. Piling in a thick layer of kitchen waste so that it begins to putrefy and exclude the air will cause this sort of problem. Adding fresh green materials that heat up as they decompose will also kill worms or drive them away.

I am going on holiday – will my worms die if not fed?
An established worm bin can be left for up to four weeks with no adverse effects if you feed the worms well before you leave. Left for longer periods the worm population would slowly decline.

How would you rate this page?
◉ Boring ◉ Interesting
◉ Useful ◉ Fascinating
Vote NOW

Dictionary check

composting the process of decomposing organic substances to create manure
putrefy to rot

Exploring presentational features

The writer of this website uses different features in order to present the explanation clearly for the reader.

- **Headings** are used to organise the text into different sections, breaking the explanation down into separate stages for the reader.

- **Bullet points** are used to make the key features of the text stand out.

- **Numbered instructions** are used to ensure that the sequence of instructions given is clear for the reader and easy to follow.

1 What other techniques does the writer use in the text in order to present the explanation clearly?

2 What features of web pages would you not find in books? Can you see any of these features in the 'How to make a worm composter' website?

3 a) Re-read the sections headed 'What you need …' and 'How to make your worm composter …'. What difficulties might a reader experience with some of the instructions outlined in these two sections?

> Example
>
> *The instruction to use 'some small pieces of wood' doesn't make it clear what exact size or shape the wood should be, or how many pieces are needed.*

b) Choose three instructions from these sections that you think could be made clearer. Rewrite the sentences in order to make the instructions more precise. You will have to make up your own details.

Word level

Language change

Nowadays, when people talk about the 'net' and 'web pages' we know that these are words to do with the Internet and electronic communication. However, lots of these terms are relatively new words as they are used to describe things that have only existed quite recently. To create new terms, older words whose meanings fit the new invention or idea are often used or combined with other words.

Example

The term 'World Wide Web' was created to describe the linked network of computers all over the world. Hence the fact that most web addresses begin with 'www'. When the World Wide Web was created, somebody said that if you drew a picture with lines showing the connections between all the computers it would look like a spider's web, and this is how it got its name. This term is now often shortened to 'the web'.

1 Find out what the following words to do with the Internet mean. Then explain why you think they were given these names.

a) web browser   d) surfing

b) homepage   e) snail mail

c) hyperlink   f) download

2 Find five more examples of new words to do with the Internet and electronic communication. For each one, write a sentence explaining what it means.

3 You have been asked to create new words to describe the following new inventions. Use and combine existing words that help to describe what the invention does to create a new word.

a) A mobile phone with a navigational system

b) A mobile phone with a web camera

c) A computer without a keyboard that responds to your voice or thoughts

d) A car that drives itself on motorways

Imperative sentences

When giving instructions, writers often use a special form of the verb, called the **imperative**. The main imperative form is the basic form of the verb without any endings. Sentences that include the imperative form of the verb are called **imperative sentences.**

Example

> **Drill** some breathing holes into the lid of the bin.
>
> **Place** the food scraps on the surface.

Imperatives don't have a subject pronoun, but it is still clear that the reader is being addressed as it sounds like an order.

1 Pick out three other imperative sentences from the text and underline the imperative form of the verb included in each one.

2 Write a set of instructions for a process or procedure that you know about, such as sending an e-mail, for an adult who knows nothing about computers. Make sure that you write in imperative sentences.

Negative imperatives are made with the addition of 'do not' or 'don't' before the basic form of the verb. This type of imperative is used when the writer wants to instruct the reader what not to do.

Example

> *... but don't cover the whole surface as the worms need a small area to escape ...*

3 Look at the section headed 'What can I put in my worm compost bin?' Present this information as a set of instructions.

   a) Write three imperative sentences explaining what you can feed composting worms.

   b) Write three negative imperative sentences explaining what you should not feed composting worms.

Combining images with a presentation

You are going to work in pairs. You have been asked to make a short presentation to the rest of your class about the importance of looking after the environment. Look back at the photograph on page 53. This photograph is a powerful image that helps to emphasise the importance of caring for our environment. In your presentation you should find five or six pictures that you can show to the class that support the points you are making in your presentation.

To prepare your presentation, follow these steps.

- Look for powerful photographs that help to communicate the idea that it is important to look after the environment. You could look in your school or local library for books about the environment or search the websites of organisations such as Friends of the Earth or Greenpeace. You might want to choose images that show the impact of events that harm the environment, such as oil spills, or look for images that show how we can look after the environment, such as people using recycling bins.

- When you have chosen your images, write a paragraph for each one explaining what the image shows and how this emphasises the importance of looking after the environment.

- You should write a paragraph to introduce your presentation, explaining what it is going to be about and a concluding paragraph where you sum up the points you have made.

- Think about how you can present the images to your class as you speak. You might want to use an overhead projector or enlarge the images so they can be displayed as posters around the class.

When you have practised your presentation, present it to the rest of the class. Make sure that you speak clearly and confidently to help the class focus on the pictures, rather than you as a speaker.

Writing to explain

W Writing: minor task

Using the photographs and the notes you made from your Speaking and listening presentation, design your own web page that explains why it is important to look after the environment.

Plan out your web page on a sheet of paper showing where your pictures and text would go. Mark on any Internet features that you want to include, such as hyperlinks, and explain how these would work. Remember not to use too much text in a web page, as bite-sized chunks are easier to read.

W Writing: major task

Your website explaining why it is important to look after the environment has become so popular that your school has asked you to write an article for the school website explaining how pupils can look after the school environment.

Use the planning frame below to help you to think of ways in which pupils can look after the school environment.

When you have completed your planning, use the writing frame to help you organise your article.

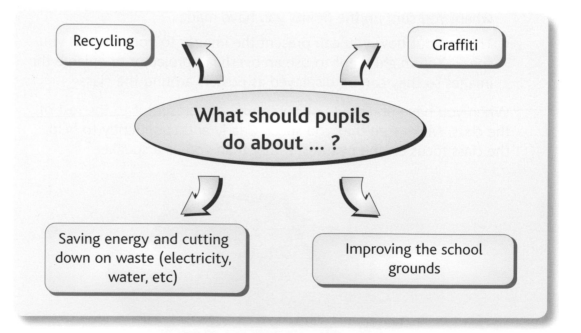

Recycling

Graffiti

What should pupils do about ... ?

Saving energy and cutting down on waste (electricity, water, etc)

Improving the school grounds

What to include	How to write it	Sentence starters
Start with a title that sums up what the article is going to be about. Include an introductory paragraph that explains what the school environment is, and why it needs to be looked after.	Make your title clear and straightforward. Include persuasive words and phrases that make it clear why it is important to look after the school environment.	**HOW TO …** **The school environment is …** **It is important to …** **Just follow the …** **You will feel …**
Include two or three paragraphs explaining what pupils can do to improve several aspects of the school environment.	Include appropriate sub-headings. These could be in the form of questions. Use imperative sentences, but also provide reasons.	**How can we get rid of …?** **• Place all …** **You should do this because …**
Give pupils detailed instructions explaining how to carry out a process for improving the school environment, such as checking whether a drink can is suitable to be recycled.	Use numbered instructions to make the sequence of the process clear. Use imperative sentences.	**1 Check the …** **2 Place the …** **3 If you see …** **4 Put the …**
Include a paragraph explaining what pupils shouldn't do in order to protect the school environment. Give reasons why these things shouldn't be done.	Use negative imperatives to emphasise what shouldn't be done. Include personal pronouns to involve the reader in the explanation.	**Don't throw …** **Don't …** **If you see somebody … , don't ignore them but tell them to …**
Finish with a short paragraph summarising why it is important to look after the school environment.	Use bullet points to make clear to your reader the main points. You could use a question and answer format.	**So why is it important to … ?** **Looking after the school environment helps …**

Help box

1. Think about where and when you should use presentational features such as **headings**, **bullet points** and **numbered instructions** in your article.

Environment Unit 7: Describe

Good writers are particularly clever at creating pictures in words, pictures that stay in the reader's mind. Some writers do this by building up layers of **description**, using adjectives and adverbs to intensify everything described, cramming in details of what things look like, smell like and sound like. The activities in this unit will help you to develop this skill, so that what you write will remain as a picture in your reader's mind, long after your actual words have been forgotten.

You are going to read an extract from *The Iron Woman*, a novel by Ted Hughes. In this part of the novel, Lucy is trying to clean from the Iron Woman the mud, slime and roots of the marshes. This is a race against time, since daybreak will reveal to the whole village the strange iron monster who is becoming Lucy's friend.

Pre-reading

1 Choose a building that you know really well but that your partner hasn't seen. Write a description of it in as much detail as you can, but using no more than a hundred words. Give your description to a partner and ask them to sketch a picture from what you have written.

2 Compare the drawing with your written description. What would you have needed to add to your description to make the drawing more accurate?

The Iron Woman

This immense creature seemed to be made entirely of black slime, with reeds and tendrils of roots clinging all over. Lucy simply stared up at the face that stared down at her. She felt a wild excitement, as if she were travelling at the most tremendous speed. Had this thing come from the sea, and waded through the marsh? She remembered the face like a seal's in her nightmare, the girl's face with eyes like a seal, and then very sharp and clear that voice crying: 'Clean me.' Had it said: 'Clean me'? Was this what the snowdrops meant?

Lucy knew exactly what to do. She unrolled her father's hosepipe, which was already fitted to an outside tap, turned the tap full on, and pressed her finger half over the nozzle to make a stiff jet.

It was then she thought she heard another voice, a soft, rumbling voice. Like far-off thunder. She could not be sure where it came from. A strange voice. At least, it had a strange effect on Lucy. It made her feel safe and bold. And she seemed to hear:

'Waste no time.'

The moment the jet hit the nearest leg she saw the bright gloss beneath. It looked like metal – polished black metal. The mud sluiced off easily. But it was a big job. And Lucy was thinking: What are people going to think when it gets light and they see this? She washed the nearest leg, the giant foot, the peculiar toes. She hosed between the toes. This first leg took about as much hosing as an entire car.

The voice came again, so low it seemed to vibrate inside her:

'Hurry!'

A faint tinge of pink outlined the chimneys to the east. Already it seemed that every single bird in the village must be singing. A van went past.

Lucy switched the jet to the face. It was an awesome face, like a great, black, wet mudpack. Then the giant hand opened palm upwards, flat on the driveway. Lucy saw what was wanted. She stepped on to the hand, which lifted her close to the face.

The jet sizzled into the deep crevices around the tightly closed eyes and over the strange curves of the cheeks. As she angled the jet to the

massively folded shape of the lips, the eyes opened, brilliantly black, and beamed at her. Then Lucy saw that this huge being was a woman. It was exactly as if the rigid jet of water were carving this gleaming, black, giant woman out of a cliff of black clay. Last, she drove the slicing water into the hair – huge coils of wires in a complicated arrangement. And the great face closed its eyes and opened its mouth and laughed softly.

Lucy could see the muddy water splashing on to the white, pebble-dashed wall of the house and realized it was almost daylight. She turned, and saw a red-hot cinder of sun between two houses. A lorry thumped past. She knew then that she wasn't going to get this job finished.

At the same moment, still holding Lucy in her hand, the giant figure heaved upright. Lucy knew that the voice had rumbled, somewhere: 'More water.' She dropped the hose, which writhed itself into a comfortable position and went on squirting over the driveway.

'There's the canal,' she said.

The other great hand pushed her gently, till she lay in the crook of the huge arm, like a very small doll. This was no time to bother about the mud or the smell of it. She saw the light of her own bedroom go past, slightly below her, the window still open, as the giant woman turned up the street.

When they reached the canal, and stood on the bridge looking down, Lucy suddenly felt guilty. For some reason, it was almost empty of water, as she had never seen before. A long, black, oily puddle lay between slopes of drying grey mud. And embedded in the mud were rusty bicycle wheels, supermarket trolleys, bedsteads, prams, old refrigerators, washing machines, car batteries, even two or three old cars, along with hundreds of rusty, twisted odds and ends, tangles of wire, cans and bottles and plastic bags. They both stared for a while. Lucy felt she was seeing this place for the first time. It looked like a canal only when it was full of water. Now it was nearly empty, it was obviously a rubbish dump.

'The river,' came the low, rumbling voice, vibrating Lucy's whole body where she lay.

The river ran behind a strip of woodland, a mile away across the fields. That was a strange ride for Lucy. The sun had risen and hung clear, a red ball. She could see a light on in a farmhouse. A flock of sheep and lambs poured wildly into a far corner. Any second she expected to hear a shout.

But they reached the strip of trees. And there was the river. It swirled past, cold and unfriendly in the early light. The hand set Lucy down among the weeds of the bank, and she watched amazed as the gigantic figure waded out into midstream, till the water bulged and bubbled past those thighs that were like the pillars of a bridge. There, in the middle of the river, the giant woman kneeled, bowed, and plunged under the surface. For a moment, a great mound of foaming water heaved up. Then the head and shoulders hoisted clear, glistening black, and plunged under again, like the launching of a ship. Waves slopped over the bank and soaked Lucy to the knees. For a few minutes, it was like a giant sea beast out there, rearing up and plunging back under, in a boiling of muddy water.

From *The Iron Woman* by Ted Hughes

T Text level: reading

Tracing the development of themes

1 Read the first paragraph closely. What has Lucy seen that makes her ask herself the question 'Had this thing come from the sea, and waded through the marsh?'

2 Read the next two paragraphs. Which three words or phrases best describe how Lucy feels when she first sees the Iron Woman?

- terrified
- wildly excited
- uncertain
- paralysed with horror
- that she was in a nightmare
- brave
- sure of what she should do next
- safe

3 What makes the Iron Woman say 'Hurry!'? Quote from the passage to support your answer.

4 As the reader, you know from the title of the extract that the metal monster is an iron woman, but Lucy doesn't know this.

a) Which sentence describes the moment that Lucy first realises what the monster is?

b) Why does it seem as if the water is 'carving this gleaming, black, giant woman out of a cliff of black clay'?

c) Why is the water described as 'slicing'?

5 Skim read the passage to find three occasions where the writer, Ted Hughes, describes the sun. Pick out these descriptions and explain his reasons for including them in the extract.

6 In the paragraph beginning 'The other great hand pushed her gently…' Ted Hughes lets the reader know just how huge the woman is. Write down:

a) the adjectives which describe the size of the monster

b) the simile which shows how very small Lucy is

c) the adverbial phrase which shows the Iron Woman's height.

7 Re-read the last paragraph closely. Ted Hughes uses three similes to convey the size and power of the Iron Woman.

a) What are these three similes and what do they have in common?

b) Think of a fourth simile that you might use, if you were Lucy, watching the Iron Woman bathe.

Noun phrases

A **noun phrase** is a word or group of words which act as a noun. You can spot a noun phrase because no matter how many words it has in it, all of these words can be replaced by a pronoun that stands for the noun.

Example

She turned and saw <u>a red-hot cinder of sun between two houses</u>.
The underlined noun phrase can be replaced by 'it':
She turned and saw it.

A noun phrase is often made up of several different parts, in addition to the main noun.

a red-hot cinder of **sun** *between two houses*

    Determiner   Premodifier   Head   Postmodifier

▶ The **determiner** comes before the noun (head). Other determiners include 'an', 'the', 'this' and 'that'.

▶ The **premodifier** is any words that come before the noun (head), except for the determiner. Premodifiers are usually adjectives. When more than one adjective is used, the noun phrase is called an expanded noun phrase.

▶ The **head** is the noun which acts as the centre of the phrase.

▶ The **postmodifier** is any words that come after the noun (head). Postmodifiers are often prepositional phrases which tell you where the noun is.

1 Ted Hughes uses many noun phrases to describe the Iron Woman. Pick out from the text:

    a) two noun phrases where the noun is premodified by an adjective.
    b) two noun phrases where the noun is premodified by more than one adjective.
    c) a noun phrase where the noun is postmodified by a prepositional phrase.

2 What is the longest noun phrase you can find in the text?

3 The following extract from the text has had the expanded noun phrases removed. Replace them with expanded noun phrases of your own.

> The jet sizzled around the eyes and cheeks. As she angled the jet to the lips, the eyes opened, brilliantly black, and beamed at her.

S Sentence level

Complex sentences

As you have learned, **complex sentences** are often made up of several clauses, each of which is separated by commas. It is possible to move clauses around in sentences to create different effects. This is a technique that writers use when they want to create a different meaning or emphasise a particular aspect of the sentence.

> **Example**
>
> The sentence:
> *At the same moment, still holding Lucy in her hand, the giant figure heaved upright.*
> (Meaning the giant stands up at exactly the same moment as a lorry goes past.)
> could be written:
> *Still holding Lucy in her hand, at the same moment, the giant figure heaved upright.*
> (At the same moment as the giant held Lucy in her hand she stood upright.)

1 Rewrite the sentence in the example above by changing the order of the clauses. Make sure that it still makes sense.

2 Work with a partner to rewrite each of the following sentences by changing the order of the clauses in as many ways as you can.

   a) The other great hand pushed her gently, till she lay in the crook of the huge arm, like a very small doll.
   b) When they reached the canal, and stood on the bridge looking down, Lucy suddenly felt guilty.

3 Decide how the meanings of each of the sentences are altered in each of the different versions you have written.

Improvising a story

Lucy arrives at school very late that day. She tries to slip in through the back of the science block but is caught by her form tutor. She tells him or her the full story of what has happened to her that morning.

Working with a partner, you are going to improvise the conversation between Lucy and her form tutor. One of you will be Lucy, the other her form tutor.

Before you start your improvisation, think about the following:

▶ how Lucy would act when she tells her form tutor the story of her encounter with the Iron Woman

▶ which of the morning's events Lucy would focus on

▶ how her form tutor would react to the story

▶ what they would decide to do.

For this activity it is important that you do not write anything down that you are going to say. If you do, your speaking will sound as if you are reading and this will spoil the effect. You can keep very brief notes, but that's all. After you have practised your improvisation, go back to the text and see if you missed out any details. Rehearse your conversation again, adding in any new information.

When you are ready, present your improvisation to the rest of the class.

Writing to describe

W Writing: minor task

Write up your improvisation as a play script in no fewer than 200 words. You can include:

- directions about how characters should speak their lines, including these in parenthesis before or after the words the character is to speak

- brief stage directions, stating where the scene is to be set and indicating any movements you want the characters to make.

Remember to set your writing out as a play script.

W Writing: major task

You are going to write a 300-word description of a person you know well. This might be a friend, a member of your family, or somebody that you admire, such as a sportsperson or musician. Your job as a writer is to describe the person in such a way that a reader would be able to see them in their mind's eye.

Make notes about the person you are going to describe using the planning frame below. Think about the special features and characteristics of the person, then think of the descriptive words you would use to describe them. Remember the descriptive details can be put before and after the noun you are describing. An example has been done for you.

Person: My grandmother		
Descriptive words	**Features and characteristics**	**Descriptive words**
gnarled	hands	like the branches of an oak tree

Use the writing frame on the next page to help you when you begin to draft your work. It is divided into three sections; you can choose in which order these will go in your finished piece of writing.

What the person looks like

- Remember that you need to describe the person in such a way that the reader can see them in their mind's eye.

- Include as many details as you can, using adjectives and adverbs to strengthen your nouns and verbs, making them really powerful.

- You should write this section mostly in the present tense.

I want you to close your eyes and think about ...

The first thing I always notice about them is ...

Their most striking feature is ... This looks like ...

What the person has done

- You should include a detailed description of something interesting that the person has done.

- Try to describe not only what they have done, but also what you thought and how you felt about their actions.

- You should write this section mostly in the past tense.

This person has ...

When he / she did this I thought ...

The time when he / she ... will stay in my memory because of ...

Why the person matters to you

- Here you need to describe not the person, but why they are important to you.

- You need to make your reader understand how you feel by using descriptive language that conveys your thoughts and feelings about this person.

- You will probably write this section mostly in the present tense.

This person is ... to me because ...

I go to see my ... when ...

To other people ... appears to be an ordinary person; to me though ...

Help box

1 Try to use **extended noun phrases** and **similes** to improve the quality of your descriptive writing.

Review of skills

Skills for listening ▶▶▶▷

You will know that it is important to be able to speak confidently, clearly and fluently in many different situations. You will also know how very important it is to be able to listen well. Sometimes it is difficult to know how to listen effectively, though the following techniques will help you to become a much better listener.

▶ Know why you are listening and **listen with a purpose in mind**. For example, when a teacher is explaining how to use a piece of equipment, you will listen more effectively if you particularly note the 'dos' and 'don'ts' of what is being said.

▶ **Share a listening task** with a partner. This is particularly useful if you have to listen to complicated information – one person can listen for particular information while the other person listens for something different. At the end you can share your ideas.

▶ **Ask questions** when you don't understand what you have heard. An effective listener will know when to stop the speaker to ask for further explanation or to make a note of questions to ask later.

The listening quiz ▶▶▶▷

Do the quiz by scoring yourself for each statement (1 = strongly disagree, 5 = strongly agree) and see how good a listener you are.

1 My friends describe me as a good listener.

2 I can remember exactly what people say to me.

3 I remember not only what I've been told, but also when I was told it.

4 If I am really interested in listening to something, I forget to take notes.

5 In discussions, if I get really involved with the argument, I listen to the words that are in my head, not what other people say to me.

6 I can listen for short periods but then I tune out.

7 When I'm given directions, I can remember the first two, but not the rest.

8 I find it hard to ask questions in case people think I am stupid.

Score of 30-40

You are a really good listener. You are able to focus on what's being said to you and understand it. You remember what you have been told and you are confident enough to ask when you don't understand something or when you need more information.

Score of 15-29

You are usually a good listener. You try hard to follow what's being said but sometimes you forget to pay attention and miss important information. You need to work on improving your concentration skills.

Score of 5-14

You need to do more to sharpen your listening skills. You are easily distracted and miss what's being said to you. Before any listening task, remind yourself of the effective listening strategies and make sure you use them.

Try this quiz in a month's time to see if your listening skills have improved.

Life choices Unit 8: Persuade

You are surrounded all day and every day by **persuasive writing**. This is writing that sets out to make readers do something they might not otherwise have done, buy something they might not otherwise have bought, or think something they might not ever have thought. To do this, writers use a variety of persuasive techniques. You are going to read a recruitment advertisement that tries to persuade the reader to choose a career in the army.

Before you read, think about whether you would like to join the army. Write down three reasons for joining and three reasons against joining.

AS A WOMAN IN THE ARMY, YOU'LL BE EXPECTED TO COOK, CLEAN AND DO THE DISHES.

What sort of woman chooses to prepare supper for one at -5ºC in a snow swept wilderness with only a layer of combat kit between her and the elements?

A card-carrying masochist? Or someone whose curiosity about her capabilities stretches just a bit further than whether she's going to make the 8.23 am to Victoria?

Let's put it another way. Could you survive one of the toughest management training schools in the country?

Could you walk for 2 days cross country with only 4 hours' sleep? Learn to strip down an SA80 rifle in less than 90 seconds? Survive 8-mile endurance runs? And still keep up with a gruelling academic schedule?

If you think the answer might, just might, be yes, we can offer you a job that's a never ending series of challenges.

Your very first posting could be as Assistant Adjutant to a regiment of 650 men. Heaven or Hell? You will probably be too busy to decide.

You might equally well find yourself commanding a platoon of 30 men or women. You will have to lead, teach, cajole and inspire them. You will have to be careers advisor, confidante and agony aunt.

Within the next few years you could find yourself in Bosnia, Kosovo, Sierra Leone, Cyprus or Brunei. (How does a stint with the Gurkhas grab you?)

Or your regiment could be called upon to join a UN contingent, practically anywhere in the world. You could be part of a team from 30th Signal Regiment spending 6 months under canvas in Namibia, helping to set up a telecommunications network across an area the size of Western Europe

Outside normal duties, you'll be encouraged to set up what we call 'adventurous training'. Stocking a trout lake in Australia on Operation Raleigh. Cross country skiing in Norway. Trekking in the Himalayas.

(One woman officer recently led a party on a 300-mile foot safari in Kenya, raising £1,300 to help save the Black African Rhino.)

Of course, not every posting involves jetting off to the sort of foreign parts that other careers cannot reach. But wherever your work takes you, new challenges and responsibilities will await you.

The longer you are with us, the greater those responsibilities will be.

Along the way you'll gain skills and experiences that will be as valuable to a company in the City as they are to 'A' Company on the Rhine or in the Falklands. (Systems analysis, petroleum technology,

surveying, electrical engineering, satellite communications: choose your speciality.)

No two officers follow exactly the same path. Personal strengths and interests will greatly affect the direction your career takes.

(A career as a wife and mother isn't excluded either. Usually, married officers are posted together. Those who choose to start a family do not have to leave, but those who do leave can come back.)

To apply for officer training, you need a minimum of 2 A-levels. You can choose between a Regular or Short Service Commission, depending on how long you want to be committed to the Army.

And, as a young officer, you will start your career on a remuneration package that makes most graduates' first jobs look miserly.

All things considered, it's no surprise we think a woman's place is in the Army.

ARMY
O F F I C E R
BE THE BEST

Dictionary check

masochist a person who enjoys pain or seeks out difficult and painful situations
gruelling testing, challenging, tough
contingent a group, part of a larger force

Identifying how key ideas are developed

1 Skim-read the whole advertisement. How can you tell it is an advertisement and not an information article about the role of women in the army?

2 Read the headline carefully and consider the pictures that appear in the advertisement.

   a) In what way is the headline surprising?
   b) What kind of life do the pictures suggest a woman might have in the army?

> The writer has included in the advertisement references to female army officers cooking, cleaning and doing the dishes – but you have to look very hard to find them. This kind of close reading is called **inferential reading** and it requires you to read between the lines because the writer does not actually tell the reader directly, but rather leaves the reader to work out for him- or herself the connection between the headline and the examples given.

3 **a)** Re-read the first paragraph and make a note of the reference to cooking a meal. In what ways is the cooking of this meal unusual?
   b) Re-read the fourth paragraph. What is being cleaned in this paragraph, and what is the technical term used to describe the process?
   c) Re-read the ninth paragraph (at the top of the middle column). This refers to telecommunications networks, which are set up using satellite dishes. How does this paragraph refer back to the headline?

4 Read closely to the end of the fourth paragraph.

   a) What answer do you think the writer wants the reader to give to the question at the beginning of the advertisement?
   b) What is the writer trying to persuade you to think here?

5 Read closely the next section of the advertisement from 'If you think the answer might …' to '(One woman officer recently led a party on a 300-mile foot safari in Kenya, raising £1,300 to help save the Black African Rhino.)' Look at the examples of army life that are being described in this section. Why did the writer choose these particular examples?

6 Read closely to the end of the advertisement from 'Of course, not every posting involves jetting off to the sort of foreign parts other careers cannot reach'.

   a) Summarise in one sentence what this section is all about.

   b) Could this section have been placed as the first part of the advertisement rather than the last?

When you are writing persuasively, you need to be careful to select only evidence that backs up your argument. At the beginning of this unit you thought about advantages and drawbacks of being in the army.

7 a) What disadvantages of joining the army are not mentioned in this advertisement?

   Example

   Long hours on duty when nothing happens.

   b) Has reading this advertisement changed any of your views?

Using context to work out meaning

Sometimes you will meet words you don't know when you are reading. A good strategy for helping you work out what they mean is to use the rest of the sentence to help you guess their meaning. This is called using **contextual clues**. Re-read the following sentences from the advertisement:

Example

You might find yourself commanding a platoon of 30 men or women. You will have to teach, lead, cajole and inspire them. You will have to be a careers' advisor, confidante and agony aunt.

One of the words you might not know is 'cajole'. The following strategy could help you to work out its meaning.

▶ Make sure you understand what the paragraph is saying even if you aren't sure what the word means.

▶ Look at the words that surround the one you aren't sure about. 'Cajole' is placed with 'lead', 'teach', and 'inspire' so it must mean something to do with these words. These sentences are all about making people do what you want them to do, so 'cajole' must mean something similar. See if the word reminds you of any others you know.

▶ Make some guesses as to what 'cajole' might mean. Choose one of the following guesses:

  a) force people to do what you want
  b) win them round through persuasion
  c) shout at people.

▶ Test out your choice by placing it back into the sentence. Does it make sense? Check your choice by using a dictionary.

1 Work out the meaning of the following words and phrases using the above strategy. First find each word or phrase in the advertisement and then re-read the sentence that it comes from.

  a) platoon   **c)** confidante
  b) systems analysis   **d)** miserly

Declarative and interrogative sentences

Two types of sentences that are often found in persuasive writing are **declarative sentences** and **interrogative sentences**. Declarative sentences are sentences which make a statement.

> Example
>
> *Your very first posting could be as Assistant Adjutant to a regiment of 650 men.*

Interrogative sentences are questions and they always end in a question mark so they are easy to recognise.

> Example
>
> *Could you walk for 2 days cross country with only 4 hours' sleep?*

1 Look again at the first four paragraphs of the advertisement.

   a) How many of each type of sentence (declarative and interrogative) can you identify?
   b) Why do you think the writer has chosen to use one type of sentence more than the other in the opening section of the advertisement?
   c) Why are questions often a feature of persuasive writing?

2 Look again at the next section of the advertisement from 'If you think the answer might …' to '(One woman officer recently led a party on a 300-mile foot safari in Kenya, raising £1,300 to help save the Black African Rhino.)'

   a) What do you notice about the types of sentences being used?
   b) This is a different pattern of sentences to that used in the first section. Why has the writer changed the pattern?
   c) On average, how many words are there in a paragraph in this section? Why has the writer chosen to write in this way? Are short paragraphs always more persuasive than longer ones?

The advertisement is written throughout in the **second person** 'you'. This gives the reader the impression that they are being talked to directly by the writer. It is very commonly used in persuasive writing.

3 Can you find any examples in this advertisement of the writer using language that sounds as if they are just talking, not writing?

SL Speaking and listening

Problem solving

Work in pairs to solve the following problem. You are an officer in the army and have been asked to select a person to undertake a difficult mission. Three people have volunteered, but you may take only one with you. Read carefully the details of the mission below.

TOP SECRET

A mission station in Antarctica has sent an SOS. The four officers based there have succumbed to food poisoning and are too ill to run the station, which is responsible for giving early warnings of nuclear attacks. The generator which powers the station has broken down and emergency fuel supplies are being used to run it, but these don't have long to last. The station requires people with technical expertise to run the early warning systems, people with engineering expertise to repair and maintain the generators and first-aid support for the sick officers.

Due to the deteriorating weather conditions (it is the start of the Antarctic winter) whoever goes out to the mission station will have to stay there for three months, confined to the base. A helicopter is ready to take you to the mission station but can only carry enough fuel to take you and one other officer. You will have to return to base, leaving behind your volunteer.

Now consider the fact files of each of the three volunteers.

Volunteer X (female)

Experience at Arctic and Antarctic weather stations.
Mechanical engineer.
Good in a crisis but less able to cope with prolonged stress.
No experience of nuclear early warning systems.
No medical expertise.
Heavy person – no medical or fuel supplies could be carried if this volunteer was selected.

Volunteer Y (male)

Nurse with substantial medical training.
Some technical knowledge of early warning systems.
Inclined to panic in a crisis but capable of putting up with hardship over a long period of time.
No engineering knowledge.
Kidney complaint means regular dialysis needed.
Light person – fuel and medical supplies could be carried if this volunteer was selected.

Volunteer Z (female)

Previously led an Antarctic mission.
Experience of early warning systems and some engineering experience.
Not a team player, but a good leader in a crisis.
No medical knowledge.
On previous mission worked with current leader of the station who would not work with her again.
Average weight – some medical and/or fuel supplies could be carried if this volunteer was selected.

With your partner, decide which volunteer you will take on the mission. You need to have three reasons for your choice. Arrange these reasons in order of priority and then join with another pair to discuss your choices.

Writing to persuade

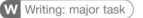 Writing: minor task

You are going to write a short explanation of your decision to your commanding officer. Text messaging and e-mail are the only forms of communication available to you. You can use a maximum of 70 words, and should aim to write in words of five letters or fewer. You can use text message abbreviations.

Write a first draft of the message including:

- a short description of the situation

- a statement of your decision

- an explanation of why you chose one volunteer instead of the other two.

When you have completed your first draft, pass your text message or e-mail to a friend to check if they can understand it. Make any necessary changes and then write it up for presentation.

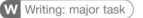 Writing: major task

You have been asked to write an advertisement on behalf of a charity, War-Aid. This charity sends volunteers to help out in war zones. Conditions are very hard, pay is very low and the environment is extremely dangerous. The advertisement should persuade young people to take up a career with War-Aid and will appear in a national newspaper.

Use the writing frame on page 82 to help you structure your persuasive advertisement. Write between 400 and 500 words.

Content	Language features	Sentence starters

Headline

Hook the reader into reading further.	Use few words Use emotive language	**War-Aid …**

First section

Establish the challenges that anyone joining War-Aid is going to face.	Include a series of questions. Select examples which are likely to appeal to an adventurous young person, using strong adjectives. Use short, punchy paragraphs.	**What sort of person …** **Could you …** **Would you be able to …** **If you think the answer to these questions might be yes, you might be …**

Second section

Describe the skills and expertise War-Aid workers will need.	Give examples and use the names of people who have achieved success. Use informal, chatty language to give the sense that the writer is talking directly to the reader.	**You might find yourself …** **You will have to …** **You could be …** **One volunteer …** **Whatever you find yourself doing, new challenges and responsibilities will …**

Third section

Outline the careers available with War-Aid, anticipating the kinds of questions the reader might have.	Use short paragraphs. Include a specific chunk of information in each paragraph.	**With War-Aid you can develop your strengths by …** **You could opt to …** **You might want to …** **You can choose to …** **For more information …**

Help box

1 Remember to write in the **second person** (you).

2 Make sure you include details of where to find out more information about joining War-Aid.

Life choices   Unit 9: Argue

There are different ways of **arguing a case**. You are going to read a newspaper article, in which two writers present their views on how television has affected their lives and argue whether life would be better without it. One of the writers supports the argument by using statistics, official sources and examples to prove how television affects people in general, and himself in particular, whereas the other writer adopts a more personal viewpoint, focussing specifically on what television has given her. Before you read, write one sentence giving your views about the benefits of watching TV and one sentence about the negative aspects.

Would all our lives be

Many of us would prefer the company of television to family and friends, according to a new survey. Women, in particular, would sooner watch telly than talk to their partner. So is TV a blight on modern life, distancing us from our loved ones? Two Express writers give their views.

YES JOHN TRIGGS

Until last week I had never tried living without television. Over the years it had become almost like a third parent to me. I had snuggled up close to it when I was a child, staring in awe at its wonders as I lay with my face just inches from the screen. As a teenager I had regarded it with typical scepticism, even though it taught me all the things about life that school and parents didn't dare to mention.

More recently, I started watching TV in a whole new way, as if this time I was the parent of a wayward child. I couldn't keep my eyes off the box, even though I often disapproved of what it got up to.

It might sound odd that I had come to see television as an extra family member but now I can at least take comfort in the fact that I am not the only one. A recent MORI poll for the Radio Times found that many people prefer the company of their television to that of their own loved ones. Some 58 per cent of women and 49 per cent of men said they would feel lonely without a TV – proof that far from being just a source of entertainment, the television has now become an essential emotional support.

What's more, 66 per cent of people living on their own prefer the company of their TV to that of real people and would rather their viewing wasn't disturbed by friends and family.

Perhaps this isn't surprising. Very clever people are paid lots of money to make TV seem more entertaining than anything our friends can come up with. They ensure it informs us without ever patronising us, makes us laugh at everybody else but ourselves and educates us without ever telling us off or losing its temper. Best of all, it flatters us. Adverts are especially obsequious – one even keeps telling me that I'm worth it.

And yet the very same study that uncovered our close relationship with our televisions revealed that almost 70 per cent of us admit that there is nothing of value to watch. Despite the programme-makers' best efforts, we don't like what we see.

We spend an average of 3.2 hours a day watching TV. That's 14 weeks a year of our spare time spent in front of the box watching what most of us agree is rubbish.

Last week my flatmate moved out, taking his TV and leaving me screenless. Suddenly I had to resort to the emotional support of real people, and it was a refreshing experience.

I talked to my friends again. I started doing all the jobs around the house that I had persuaded myself I hadn't had time to do. I went out more often, seeing people I would previously have maintained I was too tired to bother with. I seemed to have twice as much energy and three times as much time as I did when the television was in my house.

Yes, TV really is like a relative. But far from being the loving parent or entertaining sibling, it's more similar to the sort of tedious second cousin who saps your time and energy with boring stories that you still feel obliged to listen to even though you know you could be doing something more interesting. We don't like their company very much but because they've been around for so long we put up with them – but when they finally leave, life seems so much more fun.

better without television?

NO   LAURA KIBBY

Why Don't You Just Switch Off Your Television Set And Go Out And Do Something Less Boring Instead? was the name of a Saturday morning television show I would watch as a child. Despite its name, this programme was always far more entertaining than the daft alternatives it offered. It only further convinced me that television is without doubt one of the greatest inventions of the 20th century.

Without my TV I would be a duller, more bigoted, less informed, less entertained and less ambitious person. Television does not create couch potatoes, it broadens the mind. Without watching programmes about far-off places, I would not have been inspired to travel around the world. Without dramas and documentaries about other people's lives, I would not have realised the wealth of opportunities available to me and may have gone down a very different career path.

Without my favourite comedies, my own sense of humour is unlikely to have developed past rudimentary toilet humour. And without the wealth of news and current affairs shows, my understanding of what is happening in the world would be far poorer.

Thanks to television, I have seen things I could never otherwise hope to witness. I saw the Berlin Wall come down and I was able to watch Nelson Mandela being freed in South Africa. I have seen outer space and watched rare wild animals in their natural habitat.

The idea of sitting around reading or playing charades every evening like the 19th century characters in Little Women fills me with dread. It is not that I do not enjoy a good book, or am unstimulated by listening to Radio 4, or am left cold by the music on Capital FM; it is just that they do not offer the same breadth or entertainment as the screen in the corner of my living room.

Indeed, I have never allowed myself anything larger than a portable television for fear that I would never be able to drag myself away from it. Not perpetually succumbing to that favourite viewing experience, the Saturday afternoon matinee, is hard enough without having the extra lure of a widescreen.

There is nothing better than to come home at night and settle down with dinner on my lap and tune out the stresses of the day by switching on to a sitcom or period drama.

Thanks to television I share my precious spare time with faces that have become familiar and much loved because of their recurring presence in the schedules. It is like spending an evening with old friends without having to trek to a wine bar or pub. It all helps to give my life routine. And when I do meet up with friends, we already have plenty to kick off our conversations because of the shared experience of television.

When I lived alone, television made it bearable. Rather than feeling that I came home to a lonely flat, one flick of the on/off button gave me laughter and conversation. That might sound sad but it was far from it. TV gave me a psychological independence that previous generations never dreamt of. Without this fantastic invention we would still be playing dominoes every evening and moaning about our mundane existence. I know what I would much rather be doing.

from *The Daily Express*

Dictionary check

obsequious flattering, fawning
bigoted prejudiced
mundane dull, routine

T Text level: reading

Developing an argument

1 Explain how John Triggs felt about television:

   a) as a child
   b) as a teenager
   c) as an adult.

Question 1a) has been modelled for you to show you how to answer.

Example

a) As a child John Triggs tended to see the television 'almost as a third parent'. The reasons he seemed to feel this are that he found it comforting and 'snuggled up close to it', just like he might have looked for comfort from a parent, and also perhaps that it showed him many marvellous things that he didn't know.

2 Writers often use statistics (figures) to support their arguments. John Triggs quotes figures from a recent MORI poll in the third and fourth paragraphs of his article. What do you think these figures show? How do they support John Triggs's argument?

3 John Triggs begins the second half of his argument with 'And yet …'. Explain how the focus of his argument changes in the first paragraph of the second half of the piece.

4 In his conclusion to the article John Triggs goes back to the idea of television being like a family member. Explain how his attitude has changed here. Why do you think the writer uses this technique?

5 Laura Kibby, in the first half of her argument, explains what she would have missed if she had not owned a television. What positive features of owning a television are revealed in the second half of her argument?

6 What are the differences between how Laura Kibby imagines what life was like before television was invented and how John Triggs sees life without a television?

W Word level

Emotive language

The writers, John Triggs and Laura Kibby, make use of **emotive language** to convince the reader of their arguments. This influences the reactions of a reader, making him or her feel in a particular way.

> Example
>
> John Triggs describes life without his television:
>
> *Suddenly I had to resort to the **emotional support** of real people, and it was a **refreshing** experience.*

> Suggests that he had previously depended on his television rather than 'real people'.

> Implies that he was somehow renewed or invigorated.

1 Look at the final paragraphs of each writer's argument. John Triggs' begins: 'Yes, TV really is like a relative.' Laura Kibby's begins: 'When I lived alone …'

   Select words from each writer's piece which you think have an emotive effect on the reader and explain how you think the emotive language would influence a reader.

2 Look back at the sentences that you wrote for the Pre-reading activity, stressing the advantages and disadvantages of television. Rewrite each sentence using emotive vocabulary to try to influence a reader in favour of the views you express.

Both writers also use **repetition** to emphasise their viewpoints. Beginning successive sentences similarly, or repeating important words often serves to give them extra prominence and significance for the reader.

> Example
>
> *Without* watching programmes about far-off places, I would not have been inspired to travel around the world. *Without* dramas and documentaries about other people's lives, I would not have realised the wealth of opportunities available to me ...

3 What effect do you think Laura Kibby achieves by writing several sentences in quick succession beginning with the same word or phrase early in her argument?

4 Now write four consecutive sentences of your own which use repetition to stress the negative points of watching television. You could use the same sentence beginnings or you might choose to repeat a negative word or phrase in each sentence to emphasise the effect you wish to create.

S Sentence level

Conditional sentences and sequencing ideas

Writers often use certain sentence types to emphasise ideas. Laura Kibby makes extensive use of **conditional sentences**.

> Example
>
> | conditional clause | *If I didn't have a TV, I would be a duller person* | consequence clause |
> | *Without my TV, I would be a less informed character* |

The writer creates an imagined situation, life without TV, and then details the consequences of that imagined situation, in these instances becoming a duller or less informed person.

1 Find three sentences in Laura Kibby's argument which use conditional constructions and explain in each case what consequences are suggested.

2 Now write three sentences of your own, using conditional constructions which imagine the consequences of being without something important to you.

> Example
>
> *If I did not have my friends, I could not ...*

At the beginning of his argument, John Triggs organises the points that he makes about his attitude towards TV into **chronological** or **time order**. He explains that his attitude has changed over time and describes how he felt about TV as a young child, a teenager and an adult, making sure that each point links logically to the next one. This method of organisation is a good way to develop an argument, showing how time can affect your opinions.

3 Pick out the key phrases from the beginning of John Triggs's argument which indicate how his thinking about television has changed over time. Place them on a timeline to indicate when he held these views.

Past   Present

4 Write three sentences which explain how your attitude towards television has changed as you have got older. Make sure that the sentences describing your attitude are organised into chronological order.

SL Speaking and listening

Conducting an interview

Your task is to interview a few members of your class to find out how they use their leisure time, what proportion of it is spent watching television and what they like and dislike about what they see. Work with a partner and follow the instructions below:

▶ Decide what questions you will need to ask to get the information. Try to ask **open questions** such as 'What sorts of programmes do you enjoy most and why?' which allow those being interviewed to develop their opinions, rather than **closed questions** such as 'Do you watch soap operas?' which only allow a yes or no answer.

▶ Interview three or four members of your class and then discuss with your partner whether you got the answers you expected or wanted. If you did not, discuss why your questions were unsuccessful in collecting the information you required, and revise them. Try interviewing another two members of the group to see if your revised questions are successful.

▶ Finally, give a short report to the whole class to outline what you found out about how the members of your class use their leisure time.

Writing to argue

W (Writing: minor task)

Imagine you own a television station. Make a schedule for what you consider to be a perfect evening's viewing for a family. Include a mix of programmes for adults and children. You should have a good understanding of what people of your age would like to see from the interviews you conducted in your Speaking and listening task, but you must consider the needs of older and younger viewers as well.

Write two sentences describing each programme on your schedule like the TV listings in a newspaper.

(Example)

| 6.00 | **Early Evening News** A round-up of events around the world and at home. Includes news from your local area. |
| 7.00 | **Buffy the Vampire Slayer** Buffy is plagued by demons from another dimension. She finds help from an unexpected source. |

W (Writing: major task)

You are now going to write an argument saying that it would be beneficial to have a week without television. As a starting point, take another look at the second half of John Triggs's article on page 84 to see what benefits he gained from not having a television.

Use the writing frame on the next page to help you structure your argument.

What to include

- Consider here what might seem so bad to people about not having a television.
- What do you think people might most miss? What would you miss?

- What sort of things would you and your friends be likely to do? More sport? Exploring your local area? Taking up a new hobby or interest?

- What positive benefits can you see in having more time on your hands?
- More time talking to your parents and family? Spending more time with your friends?

- Try to sum up the main advantages of not having a TV.
- You might become more selective about what you watch, or may have found other things you prefer to do.

Sentence starters

Living without television for a week might seem awful, but …

This is because …

Without my television I would …

Without my television it would be possible to …

And without my television I might be able to …

Another argument in favour is that …

The reason for this is …

Even though there would be some TV programmes I would miss …

It would also give me more time to …

So, even though living without TV for a week might seem awful …

A good reason to carry on living without TV is …

But when the week is over I think I will …

Help box

1. Remember to use **emotive language** to try to convince the reader of your point of view.

2. Think about the structure of your argument and use **repetition** to emphasise the most important points.

Life choices Unit 10: Advise

When a text is written to **advise**, it will recommend certain courses of action and suggest a range of possible options, so that the reader feels that he or she has some choice over what is eventually decided. In addition, it is important that the reader has a reason to make a particular choice, and so the writer has to write not only to advise but also to inform. This means that the writer may need to provide information where appropriate and explain why particular advice is being recommended.

You will see how advice and information are provided in the text which follows. This is an article entitled 'All Over the Shop' which has been written for school leavers advising them on how they can best pursue different types of employment in the retail industry, such as working as a shop assistant in a large department store. Before you read, think about what type of job you would like to do when you are older. Where would you go to get advice about the careers that you are interested in?

All Over The Shop

There's a lot more to the retail industry than stocking shelves and till work. The demand for more motivated students in a wide range of possible careers is especially great around the Christmas period, says Jessica Moore

For a sense of autonomy and consumer liberty, more and more teenagers are looking to top up their monthly income with part-time or weekend work. Christmas is the busiest shopping season in the calendar and is the perfect time to try out a job in retail.

Yes, it's busy. Yes, it's hectic. And yes, the endlessly looping in-store Christmas carol CD will drive you to distraction, but it can also be a fun way to earn some extra cash to help make the festive season a little more … festive!

Don't just think till operator or shelf-stacker, the variety of roles and environments on offer is overwhelming. From window-dresser or layout designer to accountant or product demonstrator, the local high street can nurture your talents, be they artistic, mathematical, theatrical or social. Retail is a huge industry, with plenty of opportunities. You may even find a career.

Before you start filling out application forms and practising mental arithmetic, you'll need to know about rights and restrictions, decide what working environment suits you best and find out a little more about where to look.

Legal Regulations

Under 16s

If you are under 16, you are officially a 'child' under employment law. No child may be employed:
- If under the age of 12
- During school hours in term time
- Before 7am or after 7pm
- For more than two hours on any schoolday
- For more than two hours on a Sunday

Local authorities have powers to supervise regional child employment. They can restrict or prohibit employment deemed unsuitable or unlawful.

16–18-year-olds

If you are aged 16–18, you may be employed as a 'Young Person'. You are protected by the terms of a European Directive, implemented by UK legislation within the Working Time Regulations. There is no minimum wage for under-18s.

18–21-year-olds

18–21-year-olds are adults in law and are no longer subject to any restrictive employment rules. You are also entitled to the modified National Minimum Wage, currently £4.25 per hour. It is illegal for an employer to pay you less than this sum.

Consumer Choice

You need to decide where you want to work and what kind of environment would suit you best. Each field and environment will have its own style, sales policies and systems. You will need to ask about these in your interview, or find out by speaking to an existing member of staff. To give you a head start, here's our general guide to some of the different sectors of the retail market:

Clothes and Shoe Shops

These may include menswear, childrenswear, maternity wear, high-street chains or designer boutiques and will all demand specific skills and knowledge. It helps to have an idea of size and a sense of colour.

Audio/Visual Shops

These sell television sets, hi-fi systems and the like. Some technical knowledge is useful here because customers are likely to ask specific questions and will expect you to make assessments about which product is best for them personally. You may have to advise and recommend and perhaps even sell insurance and guarantees. Salesmanship is a useful skill for these positions.

Book and/or Record Shops

Far from just stacking shelves and working on the till, you may well be expected to have some knowledge of and interest in books and/or music, videos or computer games, depending on the department you work in.

Supermarkets and Big Stores

Supermarkets and big stores (such as IKEA, Argos or department stores) usually need lots of employees and regularly employ extra staff over Christmas and on a part-time basis. Because of this they may offer better salaries and could be more flexible with working hours and shifts.

Overall, think about how you feel about sales staff when you're out and about. We all hate the girl who shoves shoes on your feet if you so much as glance in her direction but, equally, it's frustrating when you need some assistance and there's no one on the shop floor.

Be approachable, interested, helpful and pleasant. It sounds obvious, I know, but it's amazing how many people get it totally wrong! Also, take time to familiarise yourself with what your store sells. If someone asks for the Canon X340, it helps if you know whether it's a camera or a dishwasher!

Job Search

Where do you start? The personal touch can pay off and many find that the quickest and most effective way to find part-time or Christmas jobs is to get out there and enquire.

Look presentable and visit shops you would like to work at, ask if there are any vacancies and get an application form. You may need to take some proof of identity with you (to prove your age, nationality, etc) and it helps to have a few references. If you don't have written references, make sure you know the names and contact details of people who are prepared to provide one. Try to find a previous employer. If you've done any babysitting or helped a relative with a business, even if it was just a little bit, you will have picked up valuable skills which prospective employers are keen to hear about.

Other good sources for references are teachers and family friends, who can give a character reference, or leaders of any clubs or societies you belong to. Also, type up a CV (curriculum vitae) and take plenty of copies with you to hand out.

If you're looking for jobs online, there is often an application form to fill out in place of a CV. A good place to start is www.inretail.co.uk. This site gives information about a wide range of vacancies at companies including Dixons, Gap, Arcadia (who own TopShop, Miss Selfridge, Wallis and more) and many others.

As examples, I found the following jobs advertised on this site:

Part-time Sales Assistant Selfridges London £4.65 per hour	Part-time Cashier Safeway Nationwide £ competitive

from School Leaver

Searching for essential information

Writers of texts which advise recognise that their readers may not read through from beginning to end, and may jump about, **scanning** the text to find what they want.

1 **a)** How do the sub-headings and bullet points help the reader scan the text for particular bits of information?
   b) In what ways do the different photographs give the reader extra 'reading' information?
   c) Why couldn't the text with the heading 'Paid to Play' be put at the beginning of the article?

2 Re-read the first three paragraphs of the article which aim to show young readers the advantages of working in the retail industry. What are the main advantages suggested?

3 Re-read the next section of the text from, 'Before you start filling in …' to 'It is illegal for an employer to pay you less than this sum.' What do you think the purpose of this section is? Why do you think the writer has included this information at this point in the text?

4 Why has the writer included descriptions of different types of shops and the range of different jobs and skills they each require?

5 The writer concludes the article with advice on how to get a job in the section entitled 'Job Search'. With a partner find and select three examples of good advice from this section and explain why you consider them to be helpful.

Example

Advice

If you're looking for jobs online … A good place to start is www.inretail.co.uk

Explanation

This shows where you can get further information and gives real examples of jobs found on the website, so you know it is a good place to look.

Working out the meaning of jargon

This article includes a lot of specialised vocabulary or **jargon** that relates to shopwork and the retail industry, such as 'window dresser' and 'high-street chains'. The subjects that you study at school, such as maths and English, have their own jargon, as do sports such as football with words and phrases such as 'offside' and 'penalty kick'. Jargon is words and phrases that have a special meaning in the context of their topic.

Example

> *'High-street chains' doesn't mean a chain of metal links going down the road, but is the term used to describe the major shops which have stores in many towns, such as Topshop and Dixons.*

The problem with jargon is when it is used with people who are not familiar with it and therefore do not understand it. A helpful way of dealing with this problem is to create a **glossary**.

1 The first stage in creating a glossary is to group words into different categories. Look at the following list of terms taken from the article.

till operator	window-dresser	layout designer
consumer liberty	supermarkets	product demonstrator
employers	curriculum vitae	working environment
shifts	European directive	sales policies
salesmanship	department stores	working time regulations
designer boutiques	UK legislation	industrial undertaking
shelf stacker	local authority	

Group each of these terms under one of the following headings.

Types of jobs	Types of shops	Laws related to shop work	Terms related to selling and buying
window dresser			

2 Work out the meanings of the terms that you have categorised. To do this look at:

- other words that you know that are similar to the word you are trying to work out

- the sentence the word is taken from to check that your idea makes sense

- a dictionary if you are stuck.

3 Choose three words out of each column of your table and create a glossary for retail industry jargon. Make sure you include the word class (noun, verb, etc) to which the terms belong.

> Example
>
> *window dresser (noun) – a person who arranges goods in a window*

4 Look at the names of the following jobs:

- till operator
- shelf stacker
- window dresser
- layout designer

a) What do these names of jobs have in common?
b) Why do you think we use these terms?

5 Create three new job titles for the following:

a) a parent   **b)** a teenager   **c)** a dog

> Understanding the history of a word can help us find out why it has a particular meaning. When you look at a word's history, you are studying its **etymology**. A dictionary will often help you find out the language that a word now used in English originally came from.

6 Find out the etymology of the following names of shops or types of shop. You should find out the language the word originally came from, what it means in that language and explain why you think these shops have used these words.

a) Arcadia   **b)** Argos (argosy)   **c)** salon

Creating an informal style

In order to present her advice effectively, the writer of the article, Jessica Moore, has adopted a particular **tone**, almost as if she is having an informal conversation with the reader. This is important in this type of advisory writing, as the reader needs to feel that the advice they are getting is personal to them, and the writer is attending to their worries and concerns. The writer has used several techniques to create a sense of engagement with the reader.

▶ The writer uses **personal pronouns**, such as 'you', 'we' and 'our'. These help to emphasise the relationship between the writer and the reader.

▶ The writer gives the reader **direct instructions**, such as 'be approachable' and 'look presentable'.

▶ The writer answers **questions** she imagines the reader might be asking, such as 'Yes, it's busy'.

1 Look back at the article. Pick out other examples of sentences where the writer has used each of the above techniques.

2 Choose one of the following topics and, using all of the above techniques, write a paragraph giving the reader advice.

   a) Advice for a parent about talking to a sulky teenager
   b) Advice for a teenager about coping with interfering parents

Other ways in which the writer of the article creates an informal style is through the use of **informal expressions**. These are phrases that are more often heard in spoken conversation rather than seen in writing. The use of **apostrophes of omission** and **exclamation marks** can also contribute to the informal style.

3 Look at the following informal expressions that are taken from the article and explain what each one means.

   a) 'more teenagers are looking to top up their monthly income ...'
   b) ' ... Christmas carol CD will drive you to distraction'
   c) ' ... give you a head start'

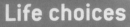

SL Speaking and listening

Discussing and delivering advice

You are going to work in a pair. You have been asked to help out with your school's careers fair where older pupils come for advice about jobs and possible careers. Because you know a lot about working in the retail industry you have been asked to advise the following three people on the part-time retail jobs they would be most suited to.

Kate

Kate is looking to earn some money to buy Christmas presents for her family and friends. She is a very sociable person, getting on well with lots of people. She is a keen sportsperson and plays for a local football team every week on Saturday or Sunday.

David

David is sixteen and wants to earn extra money to buy clothes and CDs. He is a talented musician, playing in the school band two evenings a week after a school and likes going to concerts at the weekend when his favourite bands play nearby.

Lisa

Lisa is studying art, maths and computing at A-level and is keen to work in fashion after she finishes school. Her hobbies include painting and sculpting and she is a conscientious person. She used to babysit regularly for her aunt and gets on well with children.

In your pair discuss:

- what type of shop the people would most suit working in
- the type of job the people would be best at (window dresser, till operator, etc)
- the times the people should work (Saturdays, evenings, etc).

When you have decided on the advice that you would give to each person, choose one of them and with your partner act out a three-minute role-play that could take place at the careers fair.

▶ One of you should play the careers adviser and present the advice clearly to the other person. You should try to present the advice in an informal style and explain any words or phrases that the other person might not understand.

▶ One of you should play the part of David, Kate or Lisa. You should listen carefully to the advice you are given and ask questions when you would like more information or further explanations.

When you are ready, you could show your role-play to the rest of the class.

Writing to advise

W (Writing: minor task)

Look back at the advice that you prepared for the careers fair in the Speaking and listening activity. Choose one of the people you didn't advise in the role-play and write them a short letter setting out your advice about the type of job they should do and explaining the reasons for your advice.

Set your writing out as an informal letter and remember to use the techniques outlined in the Sentence level section to help create an informal style.

W (Writing: major task)

The headteacher of your school has asked you to produce an advice sheet for new Year 7 pupils, advising them on how to cope with the move to a new school and what they should do to get the most out of the facilities that the school has to offer.

First of all, brainstorm what you think that new pupils to your school would need advice about. Think back to when you were a new pupil. What kind of advice would have been helpful to you? Use the planning frame below that suggests some areas that new pupils might need to know about to help you to record your ideas.

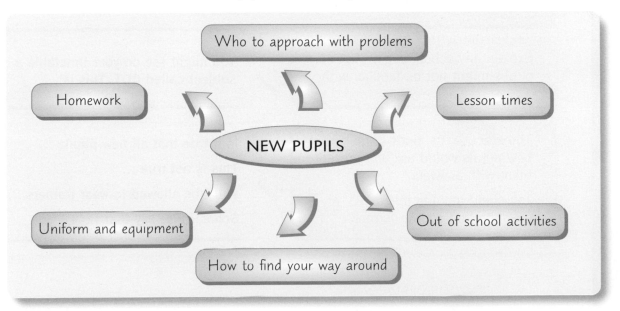

Use the writing frame on the next page to help you to with your advice sheet.

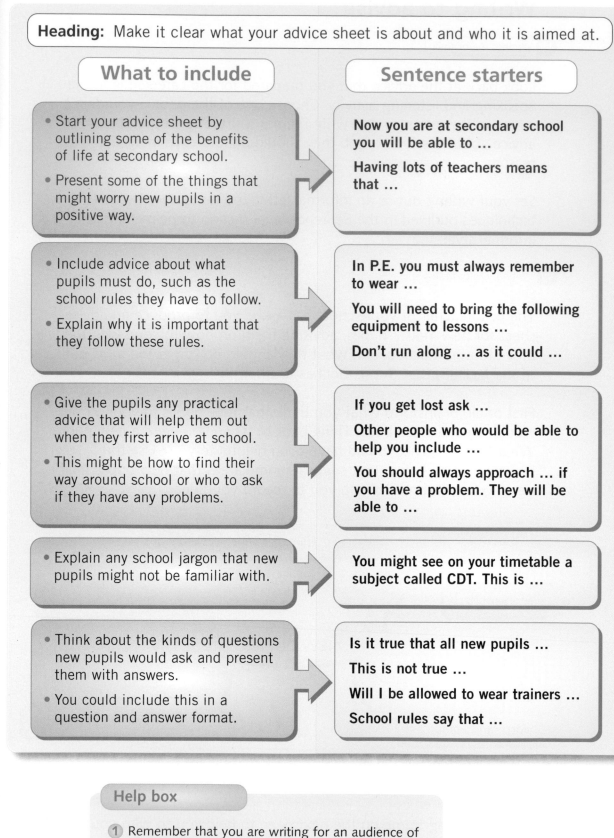

Heading: Make it clear what your advice sheet is about and who it is aimed at.

What to include

- Start your advice sheet by outlining some of the benefits of life at secondary school.
- Present some of the things that might worry new pupils in a positive way.

- Include advice about what pupils must do, such as the school rules they have to follow.
- Explain why it is important that they follow these rules.

- Give the pupils any practical advice that will help them out when they first arrive at school.
- This might be how to find their way around school or who to ask if they have any problems.

- Explain any school jargon that new pupils might not be familiar with.

- Think about the kinds of questions new pupils would ask and present them with answers.
- You could include this in a question and answer format.

Sentence starters

Now you are at secondary school you will be able to ...

Having lots of teachers means that ...

In P.E. you must always remember to wear ...

You will need to bring the following equipment to lessons ...

Don't run along ... as it could ...

If you get lost ask ...

Other people who would be able to help you include ...

You should always approach ... if you have a problem. They will be able to ...

You might see on your timetable a subject called CDT. This is ...

Is it true that all new pupils ...

This is not true ...

Will I be allowed to wear trainers ...

School rules say that ...

Help box

1. Remember that you are writing for an audience of new pupils, so use an **informal** and **friendly tone**.
2. Use **headings** to organise your advice and make it easy to read and follow.

Discussion skills ▶▶▶

Learning how discussions work, when to listen and when to speak, and how to talk ideas through are all crucial skills. But have you ever sat in a class or a group discussion and noticed how only a few people ever really join in? This means that often too few opinions are heard and opportunities to understand other points of view are missed. You will encourage others to join in a discussion if you use the following techniques.

▶ **Make eye contact** with people, perhaps smiling to encourage them to contribute. Make sure that you aren't putting other people off speaking – perhaps by sitting with your back towards them. It helps if you show you are listening, perhaps by nodding when you agree.

▶ **Ask open questions** (What do you think …? What would you do if …?). Using this type of question means that people have to reply with more than just a 'yes' or a 'no' answer.

▶ **Allow people time to think**. In discussions it is sometimes helpful to allow a pause while people gather together their ideas.

▶ **Avoid making personal remarks or criticisms** – no-one will want to talk if there is a risk that they might be hurt by what others say.

Keeping a discussion log ▶▶▶

Keeping a discussion log can help you think back to what you did in a discussion and find ways in which you might be able to talk and listen more effectively next time. Complete this talk log after your next discussion.

What was the discussion about?	
How was it organised (pairs, group, etc.)?	
What was my viewpoint at the beginning?	
What was my viewpoint at the end?	
Did I: • join in the discussion? • say nothing? • talk, but only with friends?	
Did I ask any questions: • to find out someone else's point of view? • to clarify my understanding? • to encourage someone else to speak?	
What interesting ideas did I hear?	

Media Unit 11: Analyse

Analytical writing is the sort of writing that helps the reader to understand how and why something happens. It means describing a problem or a situation concisely, making key points about the subject and then bringing those key points together into a conclusion. Analytical writing often includes quite technical language, as you will see in this article about mobile phones and the teenagers who use them. It's an article that analyses the very rapid changes that have happened to mobile phones since the 1980s and suggests the ways that they might be used in the future. Before you read, jot down a text message you might have sent to a friend recently. Then write the message in full, as you would in a note to a friend. Read the two versions of what you have written. Can you see one reason why text messaging has become so very popular, particularly with teenagers?

Teenage kicks

Teen culture has been a significant factor in the growth of the mobile phone market. Ashley Norris looks at how the industry is catering for this influential target group.

It seems astonishingly naïve now, but when SMS text messaging was launched five years ago, neither phone manufacturers nor networks expected it to be much of a cash cow. They reckoned without the millions of text message-mad youngsters who have turned two-finger typing into an artform and spawned a completely new language.

For many youngsters the mobile is the first accessory they throw into their bag; school playgrounds are buzzing with talk of the latest ringtones and coolest snap-on covers. And with innovations such as multimedia messaging and enhanced gaming set to take off next year, the love affair between teenagers and their mobiles is unlikely to cool.

● Pay-as-you-go

The catalyst for the growth in popularity of mobiles among youngsters was the development of the pay-as-you-go. Before their arrival anxious parents were more cautious about issuing phones to their offspring knowing that they could quite easily rack up large bills. The pay-as-you-go system, which at least gave the adults some kind of credit control, caused sales of mobiles to soar. This in turn inspired a massive growth in the popularity of text messaging, with youngsters eager to chat to each other using a system that was not only fun, but inexpensive.

● Customising mobiles

In the late 90s makers realised that users wanted to stamp their individuality on phones and the concept of the snap-on cover was born. Although other makers such as Siemens offer a range of covers, it is Nokia which has developed the market in Europe and in doing so established itself as leader in kids/youth phones. For budget-priced models like the Nokia 3310, 3330, and even the more upmarket 8210, a bewildering array of designs are available, from Stars and Stripes and Union Jacks to lurid psychedelic pinks and greens. Most covers cost between £5 and £20. Never one to miss a marketing opportunity, football clubs have also cashed in on the craze, offering covers emblazoned in team colours. And now phone users can show how much they care about someone by designing a cover that features their image. For £19.99 Carphone Warehouse is offering to turn a photo of your loved one into a snap-on cover for a Nokia phone in three to five working days.

● Cool ringtones

Right up until the end of the last decade most mobile phones had a rather limited selection of ringtones. The compatibility of new phones with downloadable tones, partly inspired by the success of the I-Mode system in Japan which proved hugely popular with youngsters, changed all that. Kids of all ages could now download ringtones of all kinds, from classic movie hits such as *The Great Escape* to versions of the latest chart toppers.

Ringtones have become so popular that even the weekly music magazine the *NME* publishes a ringtones chart. While Nokia was the first to develop this market, most contemporary mobiles are now compatible with downloadable ringtones.

And it's not just downloadable ringtones that have proved a hit with the teen market. Downloadable logos, which range from football teams to images of cartoons, have enabled youngsters to further customise their phones.

● Games on the mobile

Possibly the key growth area for phones next year will be games. Most models have a basic selection of rather primitive mid-80s arcade-style games stored in their memory. Nokia has increased phone-user options by offering games that can be downloaded to mobiles via the Club Nokia website (club.nokia.co.uk). Over the next 12 months those games are set to get more sophisticated, with Siemens and Motorola in addition to Nokia developing more advanced, downloadable games. The growth of Wap phones significantly increases options with users able to play sports quizzes, games such as 'Top Trumps' and versions of hit TV quizzes such as *Who Wants to be a Millionaire.*

● Text messaging phones

Phone makers have also sought to cash in on the text messaging craze by producing models which feature a mini-keyboard enabling even faster composition of messages. Sure to be the most wanted phone for youngsters this Christmas is Nokia's new 5510. This unusually shaped model with a screen between two halves of a keyboard is ideal for text-mad youngsters. Nokia has also integrated into the phone an MP3 player with storage for over an hour of tunes and FM radio. It may provide a blueprint for how kids' phones will develop in the next few years. Phones will be a great deal more than just communication tools. They will feature games, music and maybe even photo and video facilities in one device. Next year manufacturers will offer an enhanced form of text messaging called multimedia messaging, which enables the user to send image (taken by an integrated digital camera) and sound files as well as text. They won't be phones then, they'll be personal entertainment consoles.

From *G2*

Using reading strategies

This newspaper article is organised in a specific way. It has:

▶ a **headline** in bold, designed to catch the reader's attention and make them read on to find out exactly what the article is about

▶ an **introduction** summarising what the article is about and giving the writer's name

▶ five **sub-headings**, one for each paragraph, except for the first.

1 Skim read the newspaper article. Then re-read closely the first section as far as the subheading 'Pay-as-you-go'. Write down a sub-heading for this section.

2 Re-read closely the section headed 'Pay-as-you-go'. Why did the introduction of pay-as-you-go phones lead to many more mobile phones being sold?

3 Re-read closely the section headed 'Customising mobiles'. What do you understand by the term 'customising'? Write down two examples of ways in which a phone might be 'customised'.

4 Re-read the last section headed 'Text messaging phones'. Using the table below, list what inventions have **already taken place** in the world of mobile phones, what inventions **have been planned**, and what inventions the writer thinks **might happen** in the future.

Inventions that have happened	Inventions that are planned	Inventions that are predicted

5 Thinking about what you have just read, answer the following questions:

a) Do you think mobile phones will continue to appeal to teenagers, or are they just a passing fashion trend?

b) How would you like mobile phones to develop in future?

W Word level

Recognising word families

Newspaper articles about new technologies, like the one you have read, can include new vocabulary that is difficult to understand at first. One of the strategies you can use to help you with this is to learn to recognise the **word families** to which words belong.

Example

If you know that the word 'phone' is always connected with 'sound' you will be able to work out the meanings of words which belong to the 'phone family' – dictaphone, telephone, xylophone.

One way of helping you to build up your knowledge of word families is to create family lists. Work with a partner to answer the following questions.

1 a) Write the prefix 'tele' (which means at a distance) at the top of the page.
   b) Think of as many words as you can that have 'tele' at the start. Try to find at least twenty. You can swap words with other pairs in the class and use a dictionary. The only rule is that you must be able to explain the meaning of each of the words on your list. The list has been started for you.

   tele

   television
   telephone
   telecommunication

2 Create family lists using one or more of the following prefixes. The meaning is given afterwards in brackets.

   mini (very small)   super (more than)
   auto (by itself)   sub (underneath)
   hydro (to do with water)   multi (many)

3 Can you use this method to work out the meaning of the phrase 'multimedia messaging', used in the newspaper article you have just read?

S Sentence level

Control of verb tenses

In the article you've read, the writer is analysing how fast new mobile phone technology is developing. To do this, the writer describes the past (life before text messaging) and compares it with the present (customised mobile phones) and the future (video images and sound files sent with text messages). To signpost the structure of his analysis, the writer uses **verb tenses**.

Example

In the section headed 'Games on the mobile'

The first sentence is in the future tense.

Possibly the key growth area for phones next year will be games.

The second sentence is in the present tense.

Most models have a basic selection of rather primitive mid-80s arcade-style games stored in their memory.

The third sentence is in a past tense.

Nokia has increased phone-user options by offering games that can be downloaded … via the Club Nokia website.

Now answer the following questions about the section headed 'Games on the mobile'.

1 What verb in the first sentence tells you the writer is writing about the future?

2 Which verb tells you that the second sentence is describing the present situation?

3 Which verb tells you Nokia has already improved the range of games available?

4 What tense does the writer use for the fourth and fifth sentences?

5 Now look at the last four sentences of the article.

   a) Which tenses are being used in these sentences?
   b) Why does the writer use this tense?

Devising a glossary

You probably know all of the language that is associated with mobile phones, but many adults don't. Work with a partner to create a glossary for the adult in your life who still thinks telephone kiosks and heated rear windscreens are the latest technology.

1 Make a list of five technical terms you intend to include in your glossary. Glossaries have to be accurately spelt, so check their spellings.

2 Copy the table below into your book. The first word has been filled in for you, but you can replace it with your own if you prefer.

Technical term	Definition	Impact of changes
SMS text messages	*Using your phone to write messages, rather than speaking to people, by using the phone keys as a mini-keyboard.*	

3 Discuss with your partner the definitions you are going to put in the second column of the table. Don't begin to write it until you have talked through exactly what you are going to say. Make sure you discuss:

• what essential information you should include in the definition

• how to make the definition clear for a reader who doesn't understands technical terms.

4 Complete the table, making sure that you use no more than twenty-five words in each definition. Then use the information in the table to prepare a presentation, explaining the meanings of the technical terms in a clear and straightforward way.

Writing to analyse

W Writing: minor task

Completing a table is a good way of making brief notes about something you have read and need to remember. You can use your glossary as a set of notes that you are now going to develop further.

In the column of the table headed 'Impact of changes' you are going to make notes about how new inventions have changed what mobiles can do and how they can be used. Complete this column. The first example has been completed for you, but you can replace it with your own example if you prefer.

When you have completed the table, you have a set of notes that summarise some of the main ideas in the article.

Technical term	Definition	Impact of changes
SMS text messages	Using your phone to write messages, rather than speaking to people, by using the phone keys as a mini-keyboard.	Teenagers now use their mobiles to send messages because this is . cheap and fun

W Writing: major task

You are now going to write a 300-word article, suitable for inclusion in a teenage magazine, analysing a recent product or invention that has changed the way we do things. You could write about e-mail, DVDs, digital cameras, or use your own idea. It could be a new product that you own or would like to own as part of your hobby.

Use the planning frame below to help to organise your ideas before you begin to write. Make brief notes about your chosen product or invention, explaining how things were done in the past, how they are done now as a result of the new product, and how they might be done in the future.

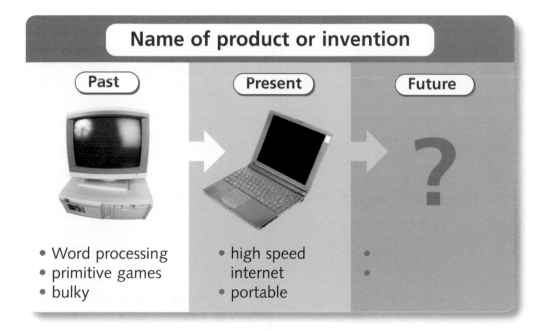

Name of product or invention

Past	Present	Future
• Word processing • primitive games • bulky	• high speed internet • portable	? • •

When you have completed your planning, use the writing frame on the next page to help you to write your article.

1

- Begin with an opening statement that makes it clear what your subject is going to be.

The invention of ... has changed the way ...

A new product on the market, called ... has transformed the way in which ...

2

- In your opening sentences, try to hook your reader's interest – a comparison of the past with the present often works well.

Five years ago ... but now ...

Once it was only possible to ... now ...

The problem of ... has now been solved by ...

3

- Now write in the past tense to describe in detail how things used to be done before your invention or product came along.

In the past ...

Previously ...

Many years ago ...

Not long ago ...

4

- Use the present tense to describe how things are now being done as a result of the invention or product.
- Make it clear to your reader whether the new product or invention is successful. Does it do things more quickly or more efficiently?

A new product, called ... is changing the way that ...

Now, a new invention means that ...

It is now possible to ...

Instead of ... it is now possible to ...

5

- Use the future tense to describe what may happen next and try to end your article with a really imaginative idea of what might be just around the corner.

In the future ...

Perhaps in ten years' time ...

It is possible to imagine that one day ...

Maybe soon it will be possible to ...

Help box

1 You might want to include some **technical vocabulary** or invent your own using your knowledge about word families.

2 Remember to concentrate on the **facts**, not your opinions. People will read your article to find out factual information.

Media Unit 12: Review

A **review** has to do two important things at the same time. It has to tell the reader what the film, book or TV programme being reviewed is all about. It also has to make clear to the reader the reviewer's opinion about the film, book or TV programme. This makes reviewers very powerful; a bad review can mean that a book doesn't sell, a film flops or a TV programme ends after one series. Reviewing your own work is also an important writing skill. Whenever you reflect on work you have done and analyse whether or not you have been successful, you are reviewing.

You are going to read a review from the *Daily Express* of the television programme *Buffy the Vampire Slayer*. The review is of a special episode from the television series, which took the form of a musical. Before you read, decide whether a newspaper review would encourage you to watch a particular TV programme. What influences your TV viewing?

INSIDE TELEVISION: TEEN HORROR
Monster Mash

DOMINIC UTTON ventures into Buffyland, only to find vocalising has replaced vampire kicking

Sure, the girl's pretty. Sure, she can fight. We know she's equally at home with sharpened stake or eyeliner, equally at ease kicking the hell out of vampires or slowdancing at the school prom … but the real question is: can Buffy Summers sing?

Screening tonight on Sky One is the first ever musical episode of Buffy the Vampire Slayer. In case you are unfamiliar with the ordinary premise of this extraordinary show, let us explain.

Twentysomething Californian überbabe Buffy, played by Sarah Michelle Gellar, is The Chosen One, the one Slayer born to every generation who is able to hunt and destroy vampires, demons and the undead.

Over the years since high school, young Buffy has achieved this with some help from a bunch of suitably mismatched school friends (including a couple of witches and an overweight odd-job man with a reformed demon for a girlfriend) and under the tutelage of Giles (the man who used to be in the Gold Blend ads, but it's never made clear whether that's a particular qualification) and an English vampire called Spike who has a chip in his head that prevents him hurting the living. He also has a crush on our stake-wielding heroine.

So in a nutshell – it's a bit silly. Naturally, then, humour is as integral to the show as suspension of disbelief – but show tunes? Now that really is hellish. Once More With Feeling is an all-singing,

all-dancing extravaganza, with the whole cast taking turns in warbling a bunch of tunes which 'express their innermost feelings'. These innermost feelings, it should be noted, largely revolve around the problems inherent in trying to lead a normal life while keeping the forces of darkness at bay.

There's Buffy singing a funny ballad about the afterlife, Spike rocking as he deals with his unrequited love for the Slayer ('I wanna be – CHA CHA – Buff-eeee's girl …'), a romantic tango from Buff's friends Xander the odd-job man and Anya the reformed demon … Even Giles shows his seductive side again with a croonalicious showstopper.

So it's all a bit silly – but then no sillier than anything else on the show (last series revolved around a Valley-girl goddess with a bad perm and a short skirt – I mean, like, really). And there's something reassuring about a TV series that is willing to take a few risks. With far too much screen time devoted to predictable and interchangeable cop-lawyer-forensic pathologist dramas, any show that's brave enough to do something a bit different has to be applauded.

Buffy has long been the best thing on television. And now it's the best thing – with songs. Sometimes you've got to ask yourself just how good can life get?
- Buffy the Vampire Slayer: Once More with Feeling, Sky One, tonight, 8pm

From the Daily Express

Identifying implied meanings

1 Re-read the headline and the sub-headings. How could you tell, before you read the review, that this was likely to be a humorous piece of writing?

2 Re-read the first two paragraphs closely. How would you describe the writer's attitude to his readers? Choose the sentence below which best matches your opinion.

   a) He wants to show that he knows a lot more than his readers do about Buffy.

   b) He is simply giving the facts about the programme to his readers.

   c) He is making his writing sound as if he actually knows the reader, as if he is writing to a friend.

3 Re-read paragraphs three and four.

   a) Whilst you are reading, make very brief notes to help you remember the main ideas.

   b) Without looking back at the newspaper review, sum up in three or four sentences the plot of *Buffy the Vampire Slayer*.

   c) When you have finished, check your summary against the review and add in anything important you left out.

4 What is the writer's opinion of:

   a) the character of Buffy

   b) *Buffy*, the television series

   c) the musical episode of *Buffy*.

   For each of your answers, provide a quotation from the passage that backs up your point of view.

5 Re-read the last two paragraphs of the newspaper article.

   a) Note down two examples of the kind of TV programme this reviewer thinks is given too much screen time.

   b) Summarise briefly what serious point the reviewer is making.

Creating new words

In the review, the writer describes Giles' song as a 'croonalicious show-stopper'. 'Croonalicious' is a made-up word, from 'croon' (meaning to sing, usually rather soppily) and '-icious' (a suffix found in words such as 'delicious'). Many words in our language are made up this way, by adding **suffixes** and **prefixes** to create entirely new words. The use of such words often has a humorous effect, as the reader is given the impression that the writer is playing with language.

1 Make up as many words as you can using the prefixes and suffixes provided in the table below. You can use any prefix with any suffix and any number of prefixes and suffixes at a time.

Prefix	Suffix	New word
non-	-est	hyperfittest
hyper-	-ese	nonactionish
mega-	-ish	
sub-	-ling	
ultra-	-able	
multi-	-ism	
inter-	-icious	
extra-	-ess	

2 Now write the dictionary entry for each word. You need to include what word class it belongs to, as well as giving a clear definition and an example of how the word can be used.

New word	Word class	Definition	Example
hyperfittest	(adj.) adjective	The most energetic person ever.	Buffy is the hyperfittest heroine around.

Creating a relationship with the reader

The writer of this review often sounds as if he is talking rather than writing to his reader. To do this he uses the following techniques:

▶ use of **colloquial** (conversational) language, such as slang, contractions 'it's' for 'it is', and abbreviations

▶ he addresses the reader directly: 'you'

▶ he includes comments in **parentheses** (brackets) that sound as if the writer is making an aside (words spoken in private conversation)

▶ his writing imitates **patterns of speech**: 'let me explain'

▶ he makes **humorous references**: 'Buffy is equally at ease kicking the hell out of vampires or slowdancing at the school prom'.

All of these techniques help to create an informal and friendly tone and help the writer to develop a relationship with the reader.

1 Identify examples of each of the above techniques in the article. Don't copy out chunks of text, just jot down words or phrases and explain which technique is being used.

2 This review could have been written from a very different viewpoint. Imagine you are writing this review for a serious magazine designed to appeal to an older audience.

a) Rewrite the first two paragraphs of the article using formal language. You can change the order of the paragraphs but you must include the same content. You could start your rewrite with the following sentence.

Example

Buffy the Vampire Slayer, an amusing programme for teenagers and young people, will be shown tonight on the Sky One television channel.

b) Now write a short commentary on how you changed the language of the review to create a more formal and serious tone.

Presenting a point of view

Work in a group of four. You have been asked to recommend the best television programme, film, computer game or book for a teenager stranded on a desert island. Choose what you would most like to recommend and write brief notes about your choice using the planning frame below. Think carefully about why you think your choice would most appeal to a teenager and why.

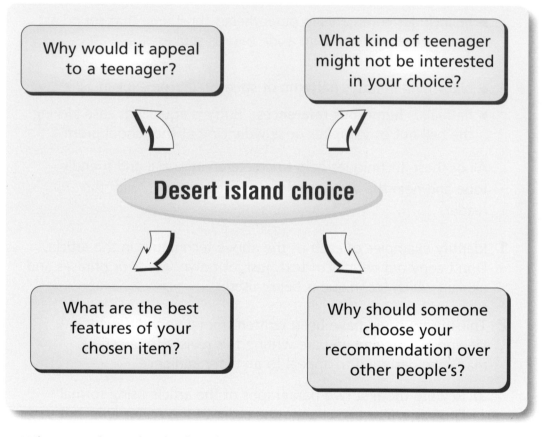

Why would it appeal to a teenager?

What kind of teenager might not be interested in your choice?

Desert island choice

What are the best features of your chosen item?

Why should someone choose your recommendation over other people's?

When you have finished making your notes, each member of your group should take a turn to present their recommendation.

When each member of the group has made their presentation, the group should consider carefully each of the four recommendations and decide which television programme, film, computer game or book they would select. It is important that you give everyone time to explain their choices and that everyone's choice is carefully considered.

Writing a review

W Writing: minor task

Decide which of the recommendations (apart from your own) that you would most like to take with you if you were stranded on a desert island. Write a brief formal letter to the person whose recommendation you chose, explaining why you decided to select it.

You should include:

- an introduction that explains the purpose of your letter
- a paragraph explaining the advantages and disadvantages of his or her recommendation
- a paragraph explaining why you selected his or her recommendation
- a concluding paragraph that ends the letter politely.

Remember to set your letter out correctly, including your address.

W Writing: major task

You are going to write a 250-word review of your favourite CD or favourite track on a CD. Your review should be suitable for publication in a teenage music magazine. Use the planning frame below to help you to get your ideas organised.

Think about	Notes
▶ who the CD or track is by ▶ when it was released ▶ what sort of music it is	
▶ why it is important to you ▶ when you first heard it ▶ what it reminds you of	
▶ your opinion of it ▶ why you are recommending this CD or track to other people	

Use the writing frame on the next page to help you. It includes a suggested word count for each section of your review.

What to include

Sentence starters

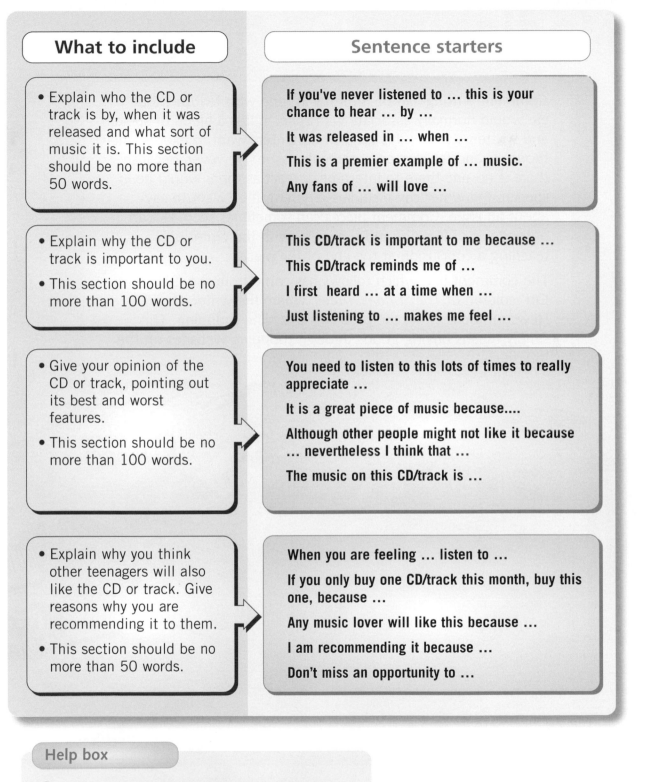

- Explain who the CD or track is by, when it was released and what sort of music it is. This section should be no more than 50 words.

If you've never listened to ... this is your chance to hear ... by ...

It was released in ... when ...

This is a premier example of ... music.

Any fans of ... will love ...

- Explain why the CD or track is important to you.
- This section should be no more than 100 words.

This CD/track is important to me because ...

This CD/track reminds me of ...

I first heard ... at a time when ...

Just listening to ... makes me feel ...

- Give your opinion of the CD or track, pointing out its best and worst features.
- This section should be no more than 100 words.

You need to listen to this lots of times to really appreciate ...

It is a great piece of music because....

Although other people might not like it because ... nevertheless I think that ...

The music on this CD/track is ...

- Explain why you think other teenagers will also like the CD or track. Give reasons why you are recommending it to them.
- This section should be no more than 50 words.

When you are feeling ... listen to ...

If you only buy one CD/track this month, buy this one, because ...

Any music lover will like this because ...

I am recommending it because ...

Don't miss an opportunity to ...

Help box

1. Try to use **colloquial language**, such as **slang**, **abbreviations** and **contractions** to create a relaxed and friendly tone.

2. Write as if you were talking directly to your reader, using 'you', 'me' and 'we'.

Media Unit 13: Comment

Comment writing can be informal in tone with features that we would normally associate with speech. It is a blend of spoken and written styles and is used when writers want to express their thoughts and feelings on a particular issue. However, because there is no one there to interrupt or react as there would be in speech, the writer can include everything they want to say about an issue. Comment pieces can sometimes seem like an outpouring of feelings and thoughts, with the writer only reaching a conclusion at the end of the piece.

The comment text which follows has come from the 'Sounding Off' column of *The Sunday Times*, where the writer, David Hewson, focusses on the problems of online shopping. This simply means buying goods through shopping websites on the Internet.

Pre-reading

What experience have you had of online shopping? Think of three advantages and three disadvantages of shopping online. Do you think that it is a good way of buying things?

Sounding off
David Hewson

Little credit for online shops

I almost gave up on Amazon.co.uk the other day. Books and CDs have been making their way to me on the web's best-known retailer for years, but then it dawned on me. Sometimes Amazon, like most Internet shopping sites, really stinks.

The latest run-in began when the site e-mailed me to say it was not shipping an order because my credit card had been declined. Funny that. It worked the week before, all the details on the website were correct, and it still cut the mustard down at Sainsbury's. I logged on again, typed in the details of a different card, Amazon pronounced it worthy and sent off the goods.

The following week, I ordered a CD. Back came the message: your credit card is invalid. Now hang on, this was the one it had accepted only seven days ago. There was nothing wrong with it.

So I e-mailed Amazon to point this out, and this is when things become annoying. Some customer-service drone replies without even bothering to read my message. I receive the same standard letter telling me how to enter card details. In fact, it takes no fewer than three e-mails before someone finally sees my point. Which is, naturally, that this is Amazon's problem, not mine.

This is all too familiar. Web shopping is riddled with niggling annoyances. Why is it that, when I order two items in quick succession, Amazon, contrary to the promise made on the site, ships them separately and stiffs me twice for the postage? Why, when I seek an explanation for its dogged insistence on downloading RealPlayer for sound clips, does it e-mail back instructions on how to download the blasted software, instead of answering the question?

Today, I actually shop online less than I used to. For one thing, the novelty has worn off. More importantly, I have come to the conclusion that many companies trying to flog their wares on the web are badly organised and unresponsive.

Take the auction site QXL. There used to be some bargains there. Now it looks like a car-boot sale laden with dismal second-hand goods. I also gave up on the travel site Ebookers. Buying air fares on the web through Expedia (www.expedia.co.uk) is great: slick, simple and fast. But what Expedia does in a couple of clicks, Ebookers only manages to achieve with several tedious steps. Why bother? The prices are usually the same.

Online grocery shopping? Not for me. No sane person has someone else choose their meat and veg for them. I had to issue a strict 'no substitutions' order, too, or risk being sent Mother's Pride instead of organic baguettes on the grounds that they are all bread anyway.

Some sites do work. Dabs (www.dabs.com) always has great prices and swift delivery on computer kit. Buying musical equipment online is also impressive. There is nowhere finer to purchase good guitar strings than Highly Strung (www.highlystrung.net) or, for those in the market for anything from a portable keyboard to a drum kit, try Sounds Live (www.soundslive.co.uk).

These places all save you money and, just as important, deliver the goods efficiently. That is the root of my problem with sites such as Amazon. The proposition it makes is attractive: go to a website, browse a catalogue of items, point at the ones you want, then sit back and wait for them to come through the post.

Then something goes wrong with the computer system. An item advertised as being available within three to four days actually takes three to four weeks to arrive. Too often the system simply does not work, and when you try to contact them, all you receive is lots of fluffy replies from people who seem to spend their working lives trying to ignore what you say to them.

Will I give up on Amazon? Probably not. On form, it is excellent. But if it cannot handle a simple credit card, it looks as if it may well give up on me.

From *The Sunday Times*

Exploring a comment text

1 The writer lets the reader know what he feels about online shopping, then details all the reasons why, before arriving at a conclusion in the final paragraph. Write summary sentences for the paragraphs detailed below. Doing this will help you to track the development of the writer's comments.

Paragraph 1	*The writer states that he has lost confidence in the Internet shopping site, Amazon*
Paragraphs 2–4	
Paragraphs 5–6	
Paragraphs 7–9	
Paragraphs 10–12	

2 Can you spot any connections between the first and final paragraphs?

One of the ways the writer adds to the informal tone he uses in the text is through his use of **word play**. He plays on the fact that a word or phrase can have more than one meaning. This type of play on words is known as a **pun**.

> Example
>
> *Little Credit for Online Shops*

Here the writer creates a pun with his use of the word 'credit' in the headline. This can be read to mean that some online shops cannot be given any credit (praise) because they provide poor service, but also can also be read as meaning they cannot handle credit card payments.

3 Work out the double meanings of the puns in the sentences below. You may need to use a dictionary.

a) Some customer-service drone replies without even bothering to read my message.

b) There is nowhere finer to purchase good guitar strings than Highly Strung.

In this text, the writer often uses **rhetorical questions**. These are questions that the writer does not expect an answer to, as he will go on to answer the question himself.

Example

Online grocery shopping? Not for me.

4 Scan through the text to find some more examples of rhetorical questions. Why are they used in this kind of text?

W Word level

Denotation and connotation

When we want to find out the meaning of the word we look at its dictionary definition. This is the **denotation** of the word. However, a large number of words carry extra meaning because they have particular connotations. The **connotation** of a word means its personal and emotional meaning. Writers use words that have strong connotations to influence the reader.

Example

To describe a conversation, we could use the word 'chat' which has positive connotations and makes the conversation sound open and relaxed. However, if we used the word 'gossip', this has negative connotations and creates a feeling that the conversation is nasty and secretive.

1 With a partner look at the phrases below that have been taken from the text. What connotations do you think they have?

a) standard letter   **c)** second-hand goods
b) car-boot sale   **d)** fluffy replies

2 Look at names of the following companies and products. For each one, write down what you feel are the connotations of the words.

a) Amazon   **c)** Mother's Pride
b) Rolls Royce   **d)** Skoda

3 With a partner, create your own name for an Internet shopping website. Try to choose words that have positive connotations. Then write a brief explanation of the connotations that it has.

Grouping sentences into paragraphs

The commentary about his experience that David Hewson gives in the text 'Little credit for online shops' is very clearly organised and developed. Each paragraph contains a major point that the writer wishes to make and each point is supported or extended by additional sentences in the paragraph. One of the main ways in which the writer does this is by adding exemplification – giving an example with some explanatory detail that backs up the main point.

Example

This is all too familiar. Web shopping is riddled with niggling annoyances. Why is it that, when I order two items in quick succession, Amazon, contrary to the promises made on the site, ships them separately and stiffs me twice for the postage? Why, when I seek an explanation for its dogged insistence on downloading RealPlayer for sound clips, does it e-mail back instructions on how to download the blasted software, instead of answering the question?

main point

Exemplification of main point

Additional exemplification of main point

Another way the writer does this is by making comparisons – including comparisons that help to illustrate the main point.

Example

Take the auction site QXL. There used to be some bargains there. Now it looks like a car-boot sale laden with dismal second-hand goods. I also gave up on the travel site Ebookers. Buying air fares on the web through Expedia (www.expedia.co.uk) is great: slick, simple and fast. But what Expedia does in a couple of clicks, Ebookers only manages to achieve with several tedious steps. Why bother? The prices are usually the same.

Comparison of how QXL used to be with how it is now

Comparison of effective travel web site with ineffective travel web site

1 Re-read the text carefully, looking for paragraphs that use these techniques.

a) Copy out a paragraph from the text where the main point is supported by sentences that add exemplification. Then annotate it in the same way as the above example.

b) Copy out another paragraph from the text where the main point is supported by sentences that make comparisons. Then annotate it in the same way.

2 a) Write a paragraph commenting on the amount of homework pupils receive, making sure the main point is supported by sentences that add exemplification.

b) Rewrite the paragraph by using sentences that make comparisons

Paragraphs also need to be linked in some way so that the reader can connect up the different stages of the writer's thinking. Amongst the useful devices for joining a text together are words or phrases known as **connectives**, such as 'furthermore', 'anyway' and 'on the other hand'.

Other ways of connecting a text together for the reader are less obvious, such as ensuring that what is written about towards the end of a paragraph is immediately picked up at the beginning of the next.

Example

The fourth paragraph ends:
Which is, naturally, that this is Amazon's problem, not mine.

The fifth paragraph begins:
This is all too familiar.

3 Write a sentence to link the two paragraphs below.

School meals could definitely be improved. For a start, there needs to be more time allocated for the lunch hour, and more assistants employed. You can sometimes wait in the dinner queue for over 30 minutes because there is only one harassed lunchtime assistant working flat out to deal with about a hundred pupils. The poor organisation of the lunch hour means that we hardly have any time left to relax or socialise.

There needs to be more time off for pupils during the school day – just like teachers. We rush from one lesson to the next and never have a chance just to talk to other pupils about things or to catch up on odd bits of homework.

Using prompt cards to give a talk

You have been given the opportunity to 'sound off' about a particular aspect of school life that you think would benefit from improvement. You have been allocated five minutes at the next school governors' meeting to present your comments. You will be working mainly on your own but do need to have a partner you can share ideas with at various points in the activity.

When giving a talk, people often use reminder or prompt cards. These are cards (often postcard sized) used by speakers to help them order and remember key points. These cards should not have too much written down because the speaker would not have time to read it, so only words, phrases and perhaps the odd sentence should be used. Devices such as boxes, bullet points, underlining and highlighting will help the speaker see at a quick glance what it is they have to remember.

When you are preparing your comments you will need to:

▶ Decide the area which you would like to 'sound off' about. This could be homework, exams, school uniform or your own idea. Brainstorm the comments that you will make, but remember these will need to be backed up by explanation and examples.

▶ Think about how you are going to structure your talk. You could perhaps use five or six prompt cards, each one covering a stage in the speech. You should write in the main point, some examples and include some emotive words.

▶ Think about how you are going to link points. You might want to include a rhetorical question to introduce some of your points.

▶ See if your partner can work out what your talk is going to be about just by looking at your notes on the prompt cards.

▶ When you practise your talk, your partner should listen carefully and make a note of which points they think would benefit from improvement. Use their advice to make any necessary changes to your talk.

When you are ready, present your 'sounding off' talk to the rest of the class.

Writing to comment

 Writing: minor task

The editor of your school magazine is keen that other pupils should read about what was said in the governors' meeting and has asked you to write a short report of your talk under the headline, 'Year 8 Pupils Tell Governors How They Feel'.

Your report should be no more than 15–20 lines long.

W Writing: major task

The next edition of the school magazine is to include a 'sounding off' column so that pupils can comment on a range of issues, such as the theft of mobile phones, local sports facilities for skateboarders, cruelty to animals, or any other issue that they feel strongly about.

Write a column for the school magazine, sounding off about an issue that you feel strongly about. Use the writing frame on the next page to help you organise your writing.

The Student Times

Sounding Off

Content	Language features	Sentence starters

Headline

- Start with a headline which will sum up how you feel about your issue.

Try to use a pun in your headline.

Sounding off about …

Introduction

- Tell the reader what the column is going to be about.

Capture the reader's interest in the issue by including words and phrases which have strong connotations.

I'm really getting fed up by …

… is beyond a joke.

Example 1

- Explain for the reader why you are interested in or concerned by this issue.

You might want to start with a rhetorical question. Try to include some speech-like phrases.

Why do I feel like this?

Now you might be thinking why is he or she thinking this?

Well, let me tell you what happened …

Example 2

- Give another example that shows why you feel the way you do about the issue.

Remember to use a sentence to link this paragraph with the previous one. You might want to use another pun.

If you think I'm exaggerating, let me tell you about …

Another thing is …

Summary

- Sum up the points that you have made and let the reader know that you have reached a conclusion.

Try to link this back to the beginning of your column. You could end with a rhetorical question.

So am I still fed up about …

Will things ever change?

Help box

1. Remember to use **connectives** to link your comments.
2. You should write using an **informal tone**.

Skills for reading ▶▶▶

We use different reading strategies depending on what we are reading. If you need to find something in a dictionary you don't read the whole of it, you scan the pages quickly to find the right word. You will become a much more effective reader if you know which of the following reading strategies you can use and when you need to use them.

▶ **Previewing**: This strategy is where you look at a text to identify how it is organised and predict what it is likely to be about. For example, when you choose a book to read, you look at the cover, the blurb and the author's name. This is the process of previewing the text – deciding whether it's suitable for your needs.

▶ **Scanning**: This is when you let your eyes 'run over' a text looking for particular information which, when you have found it, you will stop and look at closely. You scan when you are looking for the details of a particular TV programme in a TV guide.

▶ **Skimming**: This is the process of reading rapidly to grasp the sense of what's being read rather than the detail. It is an essential skill, especially in tests when you need to find out how many questions you have to answer.

▶ **Close reading**: This strategy should be used when you need to look at a text very carefully. Close reading means reading more than once, going back to make sure that you have understood fully what's being said. You close read when you are asked to study a text, such as source material in history.

Choosing the right strategy ▶▶▶

Working with a partner, look at the tasks below and decide which reading strategies you would use for each task. You may choose more than one strategy.

a) You need to know if the art book you have chosen has any information on Picasso.

b) Your search engine has found two websites on your chosen topic. You need to choose the one that has the most information and is the easiest to access.

c) You are looking for a leaflet published by a group against animal testing. You have fifty leaflets to sort through.

d) You have been asked to write an essay comparing two characters in a novel, using quotations to back up your opinions.

Relationships Unit 14: Prose

This extract is taken from the novel *You Don't Know Me* by the American writer, David Klass. In this novel the writer uses a first-person narrative, adopting the 'voice' of a young boy. The extract you are going to read is taken from the very start of the opening chapter. In this section, the boy gives his feelings about life, his school and his family, and they are presented as if he were addressing his mother directly. In this way, the reader is able to learn about the boy's character and attitudes through what he says.

Pre-reading

In the opening sentence of the extract the narrator says merely 'You don't know me.' What do you think this shows about the narrator's character or the way he feels? Have you ever felt that someone didn't really know you? What made you feel this way?

You don't know me

You don't know me.

Just for example, you think I'm upstairs in my room doing my homework. Wrong. I'm not in my room. I'm not doing my homework. And even if I were up in my room I wouldn't be doing my homework, so you'd still be wrong. And it's really not my room. It's your room because it's your house. I just happen to live there right now. And it's really not my homework, because my math teacher, Mrs. Moonface, assigned it and she's going to check it, so it's her homework.

Her name's not Mrs. Moonface, by the way. It's really Mrs. Garlic Breath. No it's not. It's really Mrs. Gabriel, but I just call her Mrs. Garlic Breath, except for the times when I call her Mrs. Moonface.

Confused? Deal with it.

You don't know me at all. You don't know the first thing about me. You don't know where I'm writing this from. You don't know what I look like. You have no power over me.

What do you think I look like? Skinny? Freckles? Wire-rimmed glasses over brown eyes? No, I don't think so. Better look again. Deeper. It's like a kaleidoscope, isn't it? One minute I'm short, the next minute tall, one minute I'm geeky, one minute studly, my shape constantly changes, and the only thing that stays constant is my brown eyes. Watching you.

That's right, I'm watching you right now sitting on the couch next to the man who is not my father, pretending to read a book that is not a book, waiting for him to pet you like a dog or stroke you like a cat. Let's be real, the man who is not my father isn't a very nice man. Not just because he is not my father but because he hits me when you're not around, and he says if I tell you about it he'll really take care of me.

Those are his words. 'I'll really take care of you, John. Don't rat on me or you'll regret it.' Nice guy.

But I am telling you now. Can't you hear me? He's petting the top of your head like he would pet a dog, with his right hand, which just happens to be the hand he hits me with. When he hits me he doesn't curl his fingers up into a fist because that would leave a mark. He slaps me with the flat of his hand. WHAP. And now I'm watching him stroke your cheek with those same fingers. He holds me tight with his left hand when he hits me so that I can't run away. And now he's holding you tenderly with his left hand. And I'm telling you this as I watch through the window, but your eyes are closed and you couldn't care less, because he's stroking you the way he would stoke a cat and I bet you're purring.

You don't know me at all.

From *You Don't Know Me* by David Klass

T Text level: reading

Exploring a first-person narrative

The **first-person narrative** has the effect of bringing the reader closer to the narrator as the events are seen entirely through his eyes – it is as if the reader is being addressed personally. The use of a first-person narrative enables the reader to gain a close understanding of the personality of the narrator, as his attitudes and feelings are communicated through the way he tells the story.

1 What do you learn about each of the characters in the extract? Copy out and complete the following table, picking out quotations to support your views.

Character	Quotation from extract	What you learn
Narrator		

2 How does the narrator give information about the different characters to the reader? Why do you think the writer uses this technique?

3 Explain why the narrator describes looking at him as 'like a kaleidoscope'. Why do you think this is an effective comparison?

4 The narrator describes himself as '… one minute I'm geeky, one minute studly'. What do you think he means by this? What sort of person would be likely to use these expressions?

5 The narrator is addressing his mother in the extracts, although she cannot see or hear him.

   a) Write down the sentence which first made you aware that the narrator was addressing his mother.

   b) Why do you think the narrator chooses not to address his mother openly? Pick out some of the ways in which the narrator describes his mother's actions. Explain what these suggest to you about his feelings towards her.

6 How do you think the writer makes suggestions about the narrator's relationship with his mother by the way he refers to 'the man who is not my father', and the way he tells his mother about how this man treats him when she is not able to hear what he says?

Word level

Extending comparisons

Often writers will use a **comparison** to describe an object or an action. Sometimes, such a comparison may be extended or developed to increase the effect. An appropriately selected comparison often helps a reader to visualise circumstances more clearly. To develop the comparison, writers often select additional characteristics to build up the picture. In the extract the writer repeatedly compares the way the 'father' uses his hands to touch the narrator's mother with the way he uses his hands to touch the narrator.

Example

He's petting the top of your head like he would pet a dog, with his right hand, which just happens to be the hand he hits me with.

By contrasting the two actions, the writer helps the reader to understand the relationships between the different characters a little more deeply, showing how the 'father' treats the narrator's mother in a tender way but is brutal towards the narrator.

1 Carefully re-read the extract, paying particular attention to the description of the 'father's' actions towards the narrator and his mother. Copy out and complete the following table by picking out all the quotations from the extract that develop the comparison between the way the 'father' uses his hands towards the narrator's mother and the way he uses his hands towards the narrator.

The way he touches the narrator's mother	The way he touches the narrator
... pet you like a dog	*... he hits me*

2 Choose two quotations that you have picked out from the extract and explain the effect they have on the reader.

3 What do you think the writer suggests about the 'father's' character by the way that he develops the comparison between his behaviour towards his wife and his 'son'?

Varying sentences for dramatic effect

One way in which writers often influence the reactions of their readers is through their use of a variety of sentence types, such as interrogative sentences, or long and short sentences. In this extract, David Klass often follows a succession of short sentences or questions with a longer, more complex structure to achieve a dramatic effect.

Shorter structures can often be very forceful because they make their point very quickly and do not dwell on description. Often they are a simple expression of an action, and may contain only a subject and a verb.

Example

She ran.

Sometimes they may be grammatically incorrect and used entirely for dramatic or ironic (meaning the opposite of what is expressed) effect.

Example

Nice guy.

1 Re-read the following paragraph:

What do you think I look like? Skinny? Freckles? Wire-rimmed glasses over brown eyes? No, I don't think so. Better look again. Deeper. It's like a kaleidoscope, isn't it? One minute I'm short, the next minute tall, one minute I'm geeky, one minute studly, my shape constantly changes, and the only thing that stays constant is my brown eyes. Watching you.

a) Why do you think the writer puts the series of questions at the beginning of the paragraph?
b) What is the effect of ending the paragraph with the two-word sentence 'Watching you.'?

2 a) Rewrite the paragraph, making the short sentences into more complex sentences by joining some of them together.

b) Read through your rewritten paragraph. Explain what effect it has on the mood of the paragraph.

Another technique that writers use is **repetition** of the same sentence patterns.

Example

You don't know me at all. You don't know the first thing about me. You don't know where I'm writing this from. You don't know what I look like.

The use of repetition can help to emphasise a particular idea, characteristic or action. Repeating sentence structures can also serve to emphasise particular relationships between people.

3 Look again at the paragraph you re-read in question 1. What does the use of repetition suggest about the relationship between the narrator and his mother?

4 Write a short paragraph about doing jobs around the house. Use repetition and a variety of sentence structures to show that the jobs are boring and routine.

Experimenting with tone

Reading this extract will have given you your own ideas about what exactly the narrator is feeling. However, if you could hear the tone in which the narrator speaks, it might influence the way you thought about him. You are going to work in a group of three. Each of you should read the opening three paragraphs of the extract to the other two members of the group in a different tone.

One of you should adopt an angry tone.

- Think about varying the volume of your voice. As you get more angry, you could get louder or perhaps more cold and precise.
- Consider where you might use pauses, and take deep breaths for dramatic effect.

One of you should adopt an upset tone.

- Think about whether pauses and breathing will be useful in emphasising how upset the narrator is.
- Consider breaking some sentences up as you speak them, to make it sound as if you are struggling to stay in control.

One of you should adopt an amused tone.

- Think about whether it would it be appropriate to laugh after certain utterances.
- Consider speaking some sentences in a sarcastic tone.

When you have completed your readings, use the evaluation sheet below to evaluate your readings.

1. Which of the readings was the most effective in showing the narrator's feelings about his mother? Give reasons for your answer.

2. Which sentences were spoken particularly effectively in each reading? What was it about these sentences which made them effective in the tone used?

3. How effectively did each reading use volume and pitch of voice?
   Was this more effective in one reading than in others?

4. In which tone did the use of repeated sentence structures sound most effective? Why do you think this was?

5. In which tone did the use of pauses and breathing seem to add most to the reading? Try to explain why.

Writing

W Writing: minor task

You are going to transform the first three paragraphs of the extract from the first person into the third person, so that the narrator is telling the story about someone else. To do this, you will need to change all the first-person pronouns to third-person pronouns.

Example

You don't know him. Just for example, you think he's upstairs in his room doing his homework.

Before you start to write, think about the effect that you want to create in the opening paragraphs of the story. When you have completed this task, compare your efforts with those of a partner and discuss the effects that the changes have made.

Relationships

A monologue is where one person speaks without interruption. You are going to write a monologue to an unseen audience, telling this audience about yourself. Your audience will be someone in your year who doesn't know you very well, so you will want to portray yourself in a positive way. In your writing you will need to:

- write in the first person as if you were talking to your audience informally

- repeat sentence types for emphasis

- follow questions and shorter sentences with longer, more developed structures.

Use the writing frame below to help you.

Introduction

- Begin with a sentence which establishes the fact that your audience doesn't know you very well.

Although you don't know me, I think …

If you did know me, you might …

How you are seen

- Talk about the ways in which you think different people see you, such as parents, teachers, and friends.

My teachers think that I am …

But they're …

How you actually are

- Contrast what people imagine about you with the way you think you really are. Try to use extended metaphors and comparisons to describe yourself.

I'm a book with a plain cover, but when you open me there are colourful pictures, exciting stories …

Conclusion

- Conclude your monologue by introducing yourself or by ending on a note of mystery.

By now you should have guessed that …

Have you worked out who …

Relationships Unit 15: Drama

At the heart of **drama** lies conflict. Sometimes that conflict may involve a physical struggle, such as a sword fight, whilst sometimes the conflict may be mental or emotional, and deal with ideas such as jealousy and revenge. You are going to read an extract from William Shakespeare's *Romeo and Juliet*, which shows a family in conflict. Juliet's family, the Capulets, and Romeo's family, the Montagues, are bitter enemies, but Romeo and Juliet have fallen in love and married in secret. In this extract, Juliet is distraught that her secret husband, Romeo, has been exiled for killing her cousin, Tybalt, and this is made worse when her mother, Lady Capulet, announces that Juliet is to marry the wealthy nobleman, Paris. Juliet refuses to marry Paris, and Capulet flies into a rage because his daughter will not obey his wishes.

Pre-reading

What do you think that Juliet's feelings would be about the situation in which she finds herself? Select from the list below her three most likely emotions and give reasons for your choices.

- anger
- self-pity
- jealousy
- guilt
- fear
- confusion
- despair
- sorrow

Romeo and Juliet

CAPULET	When the sun sets, the earth doth drizzle dew;	125
	But for the sunset of my brother's son	
	It rains downright.	
	How now, a conduit, girl? What, still in tears?	
	Evermore showering? In one little body	
	Thou counterfeits a bark, a sea, a wind;	130
	For still thy eyes, which I may call the sea,	
	Do ebb and flow with tears; the bark thy body is,	
	Sailing in this salt flood; the winds, thy sighs,	
	Who raging with thy tears, and they with them,	
	Without a sudden clam, will overset	135
	Thy tempest-tossed body. How now wife?	
	Have you delivered to her our decree?	
L.CAPULET	Ay sir, but she will none, she gives you thanks.	
	I would the fool were married to her grave.	
CAPULET	Soft, take me with you, take me with you, wife.	140
	How will she none? Doth she not give us thanks?	
	Is she not proud? Doth she not count her blest,	
	Unworthy as she is, that we have wrought	
	So worthy a gentleman to be her bride?	
JULIET	Not proud you have, but thankful that you have.	145
	Proud can I never be of what I hate,	
	But thankful even for hate, that is meant love.	
CAPULET	How, how!, how, how, chopt-logic. What is this?	
	'Proud', and 'I thank you', and 'I thank you not',	
	And yet 'Not proud'. Mistress minion you,	150
	Thank me no thankings, nor proud me no prouds,	
	But fettle your fine joints 'gainst Thursday next,	
	To go with Paris to Saint Peter's Church,	
	Or I will drag thee on a hurdle thither.	
	Out you green-sickness carrion, out you baggage,	155
	You tallow-face!	
L.CAPULET	Fie, fie! What, are you mad?	

Dictionary check

bark boat
decree decision
minion servant
baggage hussy

JULIET	Good father, I beseech you on my knees, Hear me with patience, but to speak a word.	
CAPULET	Hang thee young baggage! disobedient wretch! I tell thee what, get thee to church o'Thursday, Or never after look me in the face. Speak not, reply not, do not answer me. My fingers itch. Wife, we scarce thought us blessed That God had sent us but this only child; But now I see this one is one too much, And that we have a curse in having her. Out on her, hilding!	160 165
NURSE	God in heaven bless her! You are to blame my lord to rate her so.	170
CAPULET	And why, my Lady Wisdom? Hold your tongue. Good Prudence. Smatter with your gossips, go.	
NURSE	I speak no treason.	
CAPULET	O God ye god-den.	
NURSE	May not one speak?	175
CAPULET	Peace you mumbling fool. Utter your gravity o'er a gossip's bowl, For here we need it not.	
L.CAPULET	You are too hot.	
CAPULET	God's bread, it makes me mad. Day, night, hour, tide, time, work, play, Alone, in company, still my care hath been To have her matched; and having now provided A gentleman of noble parentage, Of fair demesnes, youthful and nobly liened, Stuffed as they say with honourable parts, Proportioned as one's thought would wish a man – And then to have a wretched puling fool, A whining mammet, in her fortune's tender, To answer 'I'll not wed, I cannot love, I am too young, I pray you pardon me' – But and you will not wed, I'll pardon you. Graze where you will, you shall not house with me. Look to't, think on't, I do not use to jest. Thursday is near, lay hand on heart, advise. And you be mine, I'll give you to my friend; And you be not, hang, beg, starve, die in the streets, For by my sould, I'll ne'er acknowledge thee, Nor what is mind shall never do thee good. Trust to't, bethink you, I'll not be forsworn.	180 185 190 195

From *Romeo and Juliet* by William Shakespeare

━━◦〰〰〰◦〰〰━━

Dictionary check

hilding worthless child
smatter chatter
God ye god-den be off with you
demesnes estates
liened descended
puling weeping
mammet doll

Shakespeare's presentation of characters

1 What does Capulet say which reveals his feelings towards Juliet when he first enters? Why does he think she is crying?

2 Capulet compares Juliet to a 'conduit' in his opening speech because she is in floods of tears. To what other three things does he compare her? Why does he say these comparisons are appropriate?

3 What makes Capulet change his attitude towards Juliet? Pick out some of the words and phrases he uses that show this changed attitude.

4 What questions does Capulet ask his wife when she tells him of Juliet's refusal to marry Paris? What do these questions show about what he expects of his daughter?

5 Lady Capulet says about Juliet, 'I would the fool were married to her grave.' What do you think this suggests about Lady Capulet's relationship with her daughter?

6 How does Capulet treat the Nurse when she tries to defend Juliet? How does what he says to her reveal his opinion of her?

7 In his final speech of the extract, Capulet becomes more and more angry with Juliet. How does Shakespeare show Capulet's anger in this speech? In your answer comment on:

- the choice that Capulet gives Juliet

- what you think Capulet's language shows about father/daughter relationships at the time the play was written

- why there are lines inside inverted commas in this speech and how you think Capulet would say these lines.

Shakespearean insults

Capulet unleashes a withering volley of abuse at Juliet when she defies him. However, you may not be familiar with many of the insults he directs at her. This is because language is constantly changing. Indeed, we probably don't use the same words and phrases to insult someone that we might have used even five years ago. For example, the word 'sad' is often now used in a derogatory sense, whereas it used merely to mean 'unhappy'. Some of the words that Shakespeare used as insults are no longer in use today. These are examples of **archaic language**. Many of the insults the Elizabethans used tended to combine adjectives with nouns.

Example

wretched, puling fool

With this insult, Capulet is calling Juliet a pathetic, weeping idiot.

1 Check in a dictionary the meanings of the following insults which Capulet uses. Then write down the closest word or phrase that you think would most likely be used today.

  a) mistress minion
  b) green-sickness carrion
  c) tallow-face
  d) whining mammet

2 Re-read the sentence which begins 'Mistress minion you …' and ends '… on a hurdle thither.' Rewrite the sentence as you think it would be said today. Compare your answer with a partner's.

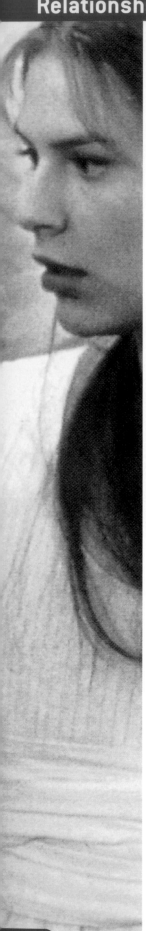

Capulet directs his insults at both Juliet and the Nurse. Those directed at the Nurse are sarcastic or comment on her interfering nature.

Example

Good Prudence. Smatter with your gossips, go.

The insults directed at Juliet tend to focus on her youth and immaturity.

Example

Out on her, hilding!

3 **a)** Make a list of three other insults which Capulet directs at:

- the Nurse
- Juliet.

b) Explain why each insult is effective in highlighting the Nurse's interfering nature or Juliet's immaturity.

4 The table contains nouns and adjectives which were used in Shakespeare's time. Make up five insults which you think would be appropriate for Capulet to direct at the Nurse or Juliet by combining two of the adjectives with one of the nouns.

Adjectives	Nouns
barren	hilding
whining	fool
puling	gossip
wretched	whey-face
foolish	baggage
distempered	wretch
lolling	rascal
peevish	cub
rascally	coxcomb
rude	
ingrateful	

Blank verse

Shakespeare wrote much of his work in **blank verse**, which is a type of verse consisting of **unrhymed iambic pentameters**. This form of verse has ten syllables in a line, starting with an unstressed syllable and followed by a stressed one. This is known as an **iambic foot**. Each line will have five of these feet.

> Example
>
> *Ay-**sir**, but-**she**-will-**none**,-she-**gives**-you-**thanks***.

In Shakespeare's plays, the characters of higher status, such as kings and nobles, tend to speak in verse, whilst the ordinary characters, such as the Nurse, tend to speak in prose. If characters are speaking words of love or heightened emotion, these also tend to be spoken in verse, as a more appropriate medium to show these feelings.

1 Say the following line aloud, stressing the marked syllables.

I **would** the **fool** were **mar**ried **to** her **grave**.

a) How does it make Lady Capulet sound?

b) Say the lines aloud again, putting the stresses on the unmarked syllables. Explain how the change in stresses alters the emphasis of the sentence and affects the meaning.

After Lady Capulet informs Capulet of Juliet's refusal to marry Paris, he asks her four questions. The way in which the interrogative sentences are structured is rather different than it would be today.

2 Read Capulet's speech, stressing alternate syllables as you did with Lady Capulet's line.

a) Which words are emphasised by the stresses? Why do you think Shakespeare decided to structure the question sentences in the way he did?

b) Rewrite the question sentences as they would be spoken today.

Directing a scene

Working in a group of four, you are going to direct a class performance of this scene.

In your group, discuss how you would direct this scene. Think about:

- what movements and gestures you would ask the actors to make
- how you would ask the actors to deliver their lines
- the reasons you would give to the actors as to why they should follow your directions.

Writing

W Writing: minor task

Re-read Capulet's final speech of the extract. You are going to write a modern version of this speech. Before you begin to write, think about how a father would say this to his daughter nowadays.

As you write, remember to replace any archaic words and phrases with appropriate modern ones. Look carefully at the changes you make and think about their effectiveness. Try to make your speech believable.

W Writing: major task

The extract ends with Capulet storming out and leaving Juliet, her mother, Lady Capulet, and the Nurse alone on stage. You are going to write a continuation of the scene, after Capulet has left.

You will need to think about the following ideas to plan your work.

Juliet's state of mind

How would she feel about marrying Paris when already married to Romeo?

How would she feel about the way her parents have treated her?

Lady Capulet's attitude

How sympathetic is she likely to be?

Will she side with her daughter or her husband?

The Nurse's position

What advice do you think she might give Juliet?

Can Juliet's problem be solved?

Dare she tell her parents about Romeo?

Would they understand her position?

Use the following writing frame to help you.

Content	Language features	Sentence starters
• Start the scene with Juliet appealing to her mother to talk to her father.	Try to use iambic pentameters to stress the important words.	**Mother, I beg you, speak to father …**
• Give Lady Capulet's response to her daughter. Is she sympathetic? Or does she side with her husband?	You could use some Shakespearean insults to show Lady Capulet's view of Juliet.	**You saw yourself your father's humour …**
• Juliet could now turn to the Nurse for help. Is the Nurse in a position to help? What advice might she be expected to give?	You could show the Nurse speaking in prose and Juliet speaking in blank verse.	**Sweet Nurse, what help can you give me …**
• Consider Juliet's response to what her mother and the Nurse have said to her.	You could again use some Shakespearean insults to show Juliet's view of the advice she is given.	**I must to clear my mind …**
• Try to conclude the scene satisfactorily. Will you reach a resolution of Juliet's problems? Or end the scene on a dramatic note?	Remember to use iambic pentameters to stress the important words that show Juliet's emotions.	**There is no means to find a way out from this mess …**

Relationships Unit 16: Poetry

Poets often choose to adopt a particular voice to give their readers a specific perspective on a subject. This can allow the reader to see things from more than one angle. You are going to read the poem 'She's Leaving Home'. In this poem, the story of a girl leaving home is presented side by side with the reactions of her parents. This enables the reader to imagine both the feelings of the girl who is leaving and those of her parents.

'She's Leaving Home' was originally written as a song lyric, and you will see that sound and rhythm are very important in the poem. You will be looking at ways in which such techniques can influence how a reader feels about the situation and viewpoints explored in the poem.

Pre-reading

Parents and children often see things from different perspectives. What things do you see from a different point of view from your parents? In what circumstances can it be difficult for you to appreciate their viewpoint, or they yours?

She's Leaving Home

Wednesday morning at five o'clock as the day begins,
Silently closing her bedroom door,
Leaving the note that she hoped would say more,
She goes downstairs to the kitchen
Clutching her handkerchief,
Quietly turning the back door key,
Stepping outside, she is free.

She (*We gave her most of our lives*)
Is leaving (*Sacrificed most of our lives*)
Home (*We gave her everything money could buy*).
She's leaving home after living alone
For so many years.
Bye, bye.

Father snores as his wife gets into her dressing gown,
Picks up the letter that's lying there.
Standing alone at the top of the stairs
She breaks down and cries to her husband
Daddy, our baby's gone.
Why would she treat us so thoughtlessly?
How could she do this to me?

She (*We never thought of ourselves*)
Is leaving (*Never a thought for ourselves*)
Home (*We struggled hard all our lives to get by*)
She's leaving home after living alone
For so many years.
Bye, bye.

Friday morning at nine o'clock she is far away,
Waiting to keep the appointment she made,
Meeting a man from the motor trade.
She (*What did we do that was wrong?*)
Is having (*We didn't know it was wrong*)
Fun (*Fun is the one thing that money can't buy*).
Something inside that was always denied
For so many years.

She's leaving home
Bye, bye.

From *Blackbird Singing* by
Paul McCartney (written with John Lennon)

Exploring the writer's presentation of emotions

1 Summarise briefly the events of the poem, as if you were telling the story. You could begin like this:

Example

Early one Wednesday morning the girl slipped out of her bedroom while her parents were asleep …

2 Why do you think the girl is 'clutching her handkerchief'? Explain why the writers have used the word 'clutching'.

3 Why do you think the girl is described as being 'free' as soon as she steps outside the house?

4 Explain why you think the writers may have repeated the words 'we gave her everything money could buy' in the second stanza? Why might this have seemed important to the girl's parents?

5 Sometimes it is possible to feel lonely even though you are surrounded by people. Why is the girl described as 'leaving home after living alone'? In what way has she been living alone?

6 What do you think the fourth stanza suggests about the feelings of the parents towards their daughter? Do you think the parents feel she has behaved unreasonably? Why?

7 What would you say is the 'something inside that was always denied'? Explain why it was 'always denied'.

Rhyme and adverbs

The sounds of words are a particularly important way in which poets can affect the readers' reactions. Sometimes, words can be rhymed to draw attention to them and stress their importance; sometimes they may be repeated for emphasis also. There are many different types of **rhyme**:

▶ Words at the ends of lines can be rhymed.

▶ A pair of lines can be rhymed. This is called a **rhyming couplet** and is often used at the end of a stanza.

Example

Quietly turning the back door key,

Stepping outside, she is free.

▶ A word inside a line may be rhymed with another word in the same line. This is called **internal rhyme**.

Example

Something inside that was always denied.

1 Find two examples of internal rhyme in the poem and explain why the rhyming words are so important in the lines.

2 Find two examples of rhyming couplets being used at the end of a stanza. For each example, explain what the effect of rhyming the two words together is.

Sometimes poets **repeat** words to create recurring patterns in their writing and to give it a sense of **rhythm**. Also where words are repeated, it serves to emphasise their importance in the mind of the reader.

3 Explain what effect the repetition of the words in brackets in the fourth stanza has.

4 Now look at the third stanza. Notice that there are no repetitions in this stanza. Rewrite the stanza, repeating what you feel are the most important lines or phrases. Explain what you think are the effects of the changes you have made.

> In the first stanza, the writers use two **adverbs of manner** to show how an action is performed.
>
> Example
>
> > *Silently closing her bedroom door*
> > *Quietly turning the back-door key*
>
> Both of these emphasise the secret and stealthy nature of the girl's departure.

5 Describe the underlined verbs in these lines using an appropriate adverb of manner:

a) Leaving the note that she hoped would say more.
b) She goes downstairs clutching her handkerchief.
c) Standing alone at the top of the stairs.
d) Waiting to keep the appointment she made.

6 Explain the effect on the sentence of each of the adverbs you have added.

S Sentence level

Tenses

> The writers of this poem give their readers two different perspectives on what is happening. This is achieved by using the **present continuous tense** to describe the girl leaving and also by putting her parents' thoughts in brackets. The present continuous tense shows an action which is happening now, and which is ongoing.
>
> Example
>
> > *Father snores as his wife gets into her dressing gown,*
> > *Picks up the letter that's lying there*
>
> The effect of this on the reader is one of anticipation, as if the action is happening as it is read and the story is unfolding in front of the reader's eyes.

1 Re-read the rest of the third stanza. What effect do you think is created by using the present continuous tense?

2 **a)** Rewrite the third stanza in the past tense.

> Example
>
> *Father snored as his wife got into her dressing gown …*

b) What difference does this make to the mood of the stanza?

Brackets are sometimes used to separate a phrase or sentence from the rest of the text when the phrase or sentence in brackets offers extra information or explanation. In this text, the brackets separate the story of the girl leaving from her parents' reactions. Sometimes we can separate phrases which are not essential to the overall understanding of the sentence, or which offer a different perspective by putting them inside commas or brackets. This technique is called **parenthesis**.

3 The third stanza deals with the girl's mother finding the letter, but says nothing of the girl's thoughts or feelings.

   a) Rewrite the stanza, adding the girl's feelings in brackets to create a contrast with those of the mother. Perhaps you could add a sentence in brackets after the third, fifth and sixth lines.
   b) Explain what you think is the effect of your additions.

Giving a monologue

The song gives us the thoughts and feelings of the parents, but we are left to speculate about those of the girl. Use the following frame to help you think about what you imagine the girl's feelings might be.

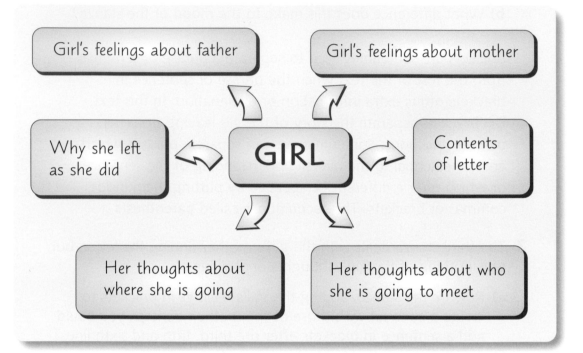

You are going to put yourself in the role of the daughter, and give a monologue, addressing your parents, to explain why you left home.

▶ The girl might not want to hurt her parents' feelings, so you might have her speaking her true feelings not directly to her parents. Just as the writers used brackets to separate the parents' thoughts from the rest of the poem, the girl's true feelings could be spoken in an aside to an audience.

▶ The girl would probably want to explain why she left in the manner she did, early in the morning. She might want to expand on what she said in the letter she left behind.

▶ It might be effective to repeat phrases for emphasis, just as the original text does, particularly when they deal with the girl's true feelings.

▶ When you are satisfied with it, speak it to the rest of the group.

Writing

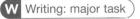 Writing: minor task

Imagine that you are going to write a novel about a girl who decides to leave home to find a new life. Rewrite the first stanza of the poem as the opening paragraph of your novel. You will need to expand on what you are given in the opening stanza.

- Describe the location to create atmosphere – the noises, the feel of the sleeping house, etc.

- You will need to include the girl's feelings – perhaps frightened, tense or worried she may be discovered. Or she may be elated when she steps outside to begin her new life.

- Think about some of the techniques you could use to build tension – use of present continuous tense, short sentences, repetition and adverbs of manner.

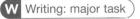 Writing: major task

You are going to attempt to write your own version of the poem, but with a difference. The original does not explicitly give the daughter's reasons for leaving, or her feelings. Your version is going to be written from the daughter's point of view.

Use the writing frame on the next page to help you organise your poem.

First stanza

... lying awake waiting for the dawn to break

... tiptoeing towards the bedroom door

... placing the envelope on the floor

Slipping ... out of the house

... shutting the back door ... as a mouse

- Place an appropriate adverb of manner in the gaps to create the feeling of how quietly and carefully the girl leaves.

Second stanza

They (...   )

Gave me (...   )

Everything that money could possibly buy

- Inside the brackets give what you think are the girl's feelings about the words outside the brackets. Don't forget to use repetition for effect.

Third stanza

- This stanza could deal with how the girl imagines her parents would react when they wake and find her missing. Try to follow roughly the same pattern as the first stanza modelled above.

- Perhaps a model for the opening lines could be:

Dad snores... [adverb of manner] as mum... [adverb of manner] dons her dressing-gown,

... [Adverb of manner] lifts the letter lying there.

Fourth stanza

- This stanza could deal with the girl's thoughts as she journeys away from her home and parents, perhaps on a bus or train. A possible model might be to give the girl's thoughts about her parents' comments outside the brackets.

We (...   )

never (...   )

gave a thought to ourselves – not a thing for ourselves

Final stanzas

- Now consider two final, shorter stanzas, which could perhaps deal with the way the girl's thoughts and feelings change from a sense of sorrow to one of elation and freedom as she begins a new life.

Skills for literacy ▶▶▶

In order to be able to improve how we write, read and speak our language we have to have a vocabulary that describes it. For example, imagine how difficult it would be to explain what you mean by a 'verb' if you couldn't actually use that word. Like all other subjects, English has a technical vocabulary of specialist words that are used to describe language itself. Your own writing will improve if you are able to discuss it using this technical vocabulary. You should:

▶ know and understand **key technical terms**, such as the names of the main types of sentence

▶ know how to construct **different types of sentences**

▶ recognise **which sentence structures to choose** for different kinds of writing.

Revising your knowledge ▶▶▶

Complete the following tasks to check how good your knowledge is.

1 Look at the following table. Decide which type of sentence each example in the left-hand column is and tick the correct box. You may find that some of the examples would fit into more than one category.

	A statement	A question	A command	An exclamation
That's a goal, surely?				
Don't touch that – it's red hot!				
Buy this computer now and save £99 on a new colour printer!				
May I stay out after 11.30 pm tomorrow, please?				
Brian isn't going to be able to go.				
I don't know what to do for the best.				
This is all for the best, isn't it?				
Stop that now, before someone gets hurt.				

2 Copy the following table that shows the different kinds of sentence structures used in different types of writing. Add your own examples to the table.

Type of text	Examples	Sentence types
Information texts	Leaflets, text books, information on the Internet	• Usually third person • Often in present tense • Combining simple and compound sentences to keep the meaning clear.
Explanations	Paragraphs in textbooks, instructions on how to use appliances	• Usually third person • Present tense for what exists now and past for what existed in the past • Use of connecting words that show the order in which things happen.
Recounts	Diaries, biographies and autobiographies	• Often first person • Past tense • Varying sentence length to keep the reader interested.
Instructions	Rules, recipes, directions	• Imperative sentences, giving commands • Short sentences giving brief, clear information.

Keep this table and refer to it when you are producing any of the types of writing it shows. You should update the table by adding information about other types of writing, such as analytical texts.